TAKING CHARGE OF YOUR EMOTIONS

TAKING CHARGE OF YOUR EMOTIONS

A Guide to Better Psychological Health and Well-Being

Louis H. Primavera and Rob Pascale

ROWMAN & LITTLEFIELD
Lanham • Boulder • New York • London

Published by Rowman & Littlefield
A wholly owned subsidary of The Rowman & Littlefield Publishing Group, Inc.
4501 Forbes Boulevard, Suite 200, Lanham, Maryland 20706
www.rowman.com

Unit A, Whitacre Mews, 26-34 Stannary Street, London SE11 4AB

British Library Cataloguing in Publication Information Available

Library of Congress Cataloging-in-Publication Data

Primavera, Louis H., 1943–
Taking charge of your emotions : a guide to better psychological health and well-being / Louis H. Primavera and Rob Pascale.
pages cm
Includes index.
ISBN 978-1-4422-5121-2 (cloth : alk. paper) — ISBN 978-1-4422-5122-9 (electronic)
1. Adjustment (Psychology) 2. Emotions. 3. Mental health. 4. Well being. I. Pascale, Rob, 1954– II. Title.
BF335.P744 2015
152.4—dc23
2015009052

♾ ™ The paper used in this publication meets the minimum requirements of American National Standard for Information Sciences Permanence of Paper for Printed Library Materials, ANSI/NISO Z39.48-1992.

Printed in the United States of America

CONTENTS

ACKNOWLEDGMENTS

The ideas expressed in this book have been influenced by many people in our lives. Dr. Lou Primavera was privileged to study with, and was supervised by, the great psychologist Dr. Albert Ellis. Many of the ideas about human functioning that are presented in this work are attributable to Dr. Ellis. The reader is directed to the appendix, which lists some of Dr. Ellis's works, and these are strongly recommended as further reading. Additionally, chapter 9, on assertiveness, is greatly influenced by the work of Robert Alberti and Michael Emmons. Their book, *Your Perfect Right*, is also highly recommended and is referenced in the appendix.

Dr. Primavera has had the good fortune to have been in contact with people of great wisdom who greatly influenced his thinking and skills as a psychologist. These people include his wife, Anne, who is the smartest and wisest person he knows. Added to this list of influential people are his godmother, Mrs. Sue Culmone; his dad, Mr. Humber Primavera; many of his friends; as well as his teachers Dr. Larry Azar and Dr. Wilfred Gibson; and his colleagues Dr. Joseph Carpino, Dr. Willard Gingerich, Dr. William Herron, Dr. Rafael Javier, Dr. Nino Languilli, and Professor Frank Slade. All have made direct or indirect contributions to this book.

As we move through our lives, virtually everyone we meet affects us. Each person teaches us something, sometimes in profound ways. Dr. Pascale's best teachers have been his wife, Lynne, and his children, Rob and Diana. Their sense of humor, positive attitudes, and reasoned thinking have taught him to be more introspective, to pay attention to how words and deeds affect the people around him, and to strive to be a better person. He also must include the various people he has crossed paths with over the years, some he has known well and some just in passing. Many have had an impact on his views of the world, often without even realizing it. Finally, he would like to thank Dr. Primavera, a close friend, a great teacher, and a wonderful human being, for allowing him to be a contributor to this work.

INTRODUCTION

This book is based on the accumulated experiences of the authors, from their many years working as therapists, teachers, and social scientists. Its main purpose is to give you an in-depth understanding of how human beings function and interact with their environment. It is not our intention to train you as a therapist. Instead, by laying out the psychological workings of people, you might reach a better understanding of how you are affected by others and your environment, and in so doing come to a better understanding of yourself.

There are many ways people can find fulfillment in their lives, but one that is particularly important to psychological well-being revolves around fully understanding what lies beneath your thoughts, feelings, and actions. It is our belief, and the belief of all therapists and professional psychologists, that we can have a fuller and more satisfying life if we can achieve a deeper knowledge of our own psychological functioning.

By gaining a better understanding of ourselves, we become more aware of how we think and what is beneath the emotions we experience. In so doing we are better equipped to handle many of the situations that can have a negative effect on our quality of life. From time to time, all of us are confronted by difficult circumstances. We might have a hard time dealing with certain types of people, have problems in our marriage, have difficulty coping with some day-to-day burdens, or occasionally find ourselves in situations where our emotions get the better of us. When conditions are especially troublesome, destructive emotions, such as anger, fear of abandonment, anxiety, among others, can dominate our thinking process and influence our actions. Some of these events can be so troublesome as to cause us to experience a sense of helplessness, a feeling that events and people control us.

Some of these situations can't be prevented. The fact is each of us faces people and situations through the course of day-to-day living over which we have very little or no control. For example, as much as you might believe it's possible, you can't control what other people say, think, or do, no matter how hard you try. When these things happen to us, we are left with finding a way of coping with them.

While we can't always control people and events, it is possible to manage some of our own thoughts and emotions. Through effective self-reflection and self-monitoring, you can develop mental strategies that allow you to control how you react to uncontrollable events. You will come to understand why you react the way you do to different situations and people. That insight puts you on the pathway to greater personal control.

Feeling in control of your life is essential for psychological well-being. By learning how to improve personal control, you will be able to maximize your positive outcomes and minimize the effect of negative ones in your daily life; you can even cope better with things that are beyond your control. You will also find that gaining more control helps you interact more effectively with those in your social world, including friends, family members, business associates, and even casual acquaintances. In short, self-awareness is the first step to learning about yourself, and that's the first step in developing the tools you need to improve how you interact with the world and enhance your overall well-being.

The idea for this book comes from an early life experience of one of the authors. When Lou Primavera was learning to drive, his instructor was his girlfriend and soon-to-be wife, Anne. He was stopped at a traffic light and he wanted to make a left turn. The driver behind him beeped his horn several times and Lou felt pressured to make the turn sooner than he wanted. After barely missing a collision, Anne asked him why he made the turn before he wanted to. He answered that he was responding to the person in the car behind him. Anne's response was straightforward, *Never allow anybody else to drive your car*. That statement has echoed in his mind for many years. We generalized that idea of driving a car to living and managing one's life. It is hoped that this book will help you learn how to drive your own car.

As you read through this book, you will be presented with true-to-life examples and do-it-yourself exercises, many of which derive directly from Dr. Primavera's experiences as a psychotherapist. These exercises are designed to help you learn various techniques and strategies to manage your life from a variety of perspectives. You will also find we repeat a number of ideas in different chapters. This is intentional because we feel these ideas are essential to the theme of the book, and if they are to be learned well, repetition is the best way for you to get there. As you come to absorbing these ideas, it is hoped you will move closer to the goal of being in control of your life.

I

UNDERSTANDING PEOPLE

Before we get into a discussion of strategies for changing how we live, we need to talk about what it means to be human. There are a multitude of theories about the nature of human beings. Philosophers, psychologists, theologians, economists, sociologists, tailors, butchers, and homemakers all have their own opinions of human nature. In one sense, we are all psychologists, even though only a small number of us have actually involved ourselves in a formal study of the field. We develop our own theories, or conceptual systems, about how people work from our own experiences, and we use these as the underpinnings to our belief systems. We then use our theory and beliefs as a guide to how we interact with other people. We can, for example, have a pretty good idea as to how someone we know might react in a given situation, or we can attribute motivations to what they say and do, as a result of our theories and beliefs about human nature.

Many of these personal theories have great value and are largely in agreement with the more formal scientifically validated theories. They give us a framework for understanding our environment and allow us to see the world as predictable and consistent. On the other hand, some of our personal theories do not have much value and, in fact, may limit our view of the world and our interactions. Prejudices and stereotypes are good examples of ineffective theories. They are made up of overgeneralized and inaccurate descriptions of whole groups of people. These are ineffective because they limit our scope of possible interactions in the world. We might draw inaccurate conclusions about a person because our biased beliefs prevent us from evaluating their actions objectively.

Presented here are the basic tenets of a theory of human nature that is based on a combination of traditional and modern views. This theory is essentially a humanistically oriented/cognitive/behavioral view of human nature. The humanistic aspect of this view assumes that people have a conscious awareness of themselves, which many philosophers refer to as the **self** or the **mind**. Humanists believe that human beings are special organisms because their essence is different from all other living organisms. They see human beings as active, thinking, and choosing organisms that have some control over their lives and behavior. This view holds that there are four major assumptions about human beings that make them unique and special, and that these assumptions play an important role in how we interact with the world:

1. Human behavior is directed **primarily** by thinking processes.
2. Human beings have freedom of choice.
3. Human beings have personal responsibility for their behavior and emotions.
4. Human beings have power over themselves and their lives.

HUMAN BEHAVIOR IS DIRECTED PRIMARILY BY THINKING PROCESSES

To a large extent, human behavior is influenced and controlled by our thoughts and beliefs. This position does not deny the importance of the influences of heredity and environment; rather, it sees them as less important than cognitive processes in determining how we act and react. Heredity provides for us our potential in terms of talents and abilities. It sets the limits for human development. Our environment can either enhance or limit the opportunities for the development of our talents and abilities. Environment provides, or fails to provide, the opportunities for us to realize and fulfill our potential that comes from the talents and abilities we inherited. Geneticists have discovered that environmental conditions can turn on or turn off certain genes. Thus, we can be born with a certain potential characteristic that may or may not be one of our defining traits depending on environmental conditions.

As one of its key features, our ability to think allows us to plan and project into the future. Thinking also allows us to be influenced by our past experiences. We carry around in our heads our personal history using the cognitive functions of memory, and we use our experiences to guide our future behaviors as well as our thought processes. It is because we store information in our brains that we have the potential to learn from our experiences.

HUMAN BEINGS HAVE FREEDOM OF CHOICE

While this idea seems simple and pretty straightforward, freedom of choice is a concept that in certain situations can be difficult for people to understand and incorporate into their thinking. We all know that in making decisions we always have options, and that our options can be limited by environment and physical conditions. You can't choose to be or do anything that you want, but in every situation you are usually faced with more than one path to take.

However, we sometimes are not aware that we can be limited by how well we understand the range of choices available to us. It is difficult to convince people who are faced with many unpleasant choices in a given situation that they, in fact, have a choice. If someone has stomach cancer, the choices of treatment, or refusal of such, are not very attractive, but they are choices nevertheless. It is interesting to note that many philosophers did not see freedom of choice as such a wonderful gift because it gave us the burden of having to choose.

HUMAN BEINGS ARE RESPONSIBLE FOR THEIR BEHAVIOR AND EMOTIONS

The ideas of thinking, freedom, and responsibility are all tied together. Responsibility implies acknowledging the connection between what we do and the results of our actions. When we choose to do or say something, we do so freely only when we recognize the connection between what we choose and the consequences that occur as a result of the choices we made.

Here's a simple example of what we mean. Suppose you decide to eat a lot of candy and as a consequence you get a stomachache. This is a true choice only if you *understand* and accept the connection between eating the candy and getting sick. When it comes right down to it, it is necessary that you recognize that you have chosen to give yourself a stomachache.

Obviously, this is the kind of behavior we expect from children and not adults. That's because very young children do not have the cognitive ability to understand the connection between what they do and the results of their actions. This is also the reason we do not hold them responsible for their actions and spend a great deal of time and effort trying to prevent them from doing harm to themselves and others. In helping children to develop, it is important for us to provide the appropriate feedback about their behavior for them to learn right and wrong, and in so doing develop a sense of responsibility.

As adults, it is our ability to make the mental link between actions and their outcomes during the decision process that also distinguishes humans from other species. If a horse kicks someone to death, we do not put the horse on trial for murder. We recognize that the horse cannot be held responsible for its actions because it is not able to think and understand, and as a result it doesn't make a conscious choice to perform a particular action linked with an awareness of that action's consequences. Certainly one could argue that a horse kicks at something as a way of protecting itself from danger, so it must understand there are consequences to its behavior. However, kicking is an innate response and not a conscious choice.

While we're typically better at it than children and animals, even as adults we're sometimes not able to foresee all the consequences of our own actions. If we acknowledge that free choice is linked to understanding consequences, when our understanding is limited then so is our freedom. Of course, our ability to achieve certain outcomes and our freedom can be limited by physical reality. For example, we can't choose to fly without a plane. But apart from the impossible, regardless of whether or not we're fully aware of all outcomes, we are still responsible for these outcomes when we make our decisions.

It is important to point out that there is a difference between responsibility and blame. Responsibility is an understanding that there are consequences to your actions. Blame implies a punitive and negative response to these actions. Sometimes blame comes from other people. We may do or say something that causes pain or harm to others. Even though that was not our intention, we have to accept the responsibility and be willing to suffer the consequences. This is reasonable, and it is one of the founding principles of a legal system in any society.

Blame can also come from within. Self-blame is a major cause of much of the depression and anxiety in the world because it leads to guilt, a harmful emotion. Guilt is like physical pain. Its positive function is to warn us that there is something that needs our attention. If we've said or done something that is wrong, guilt makes us think twice about doing the same thing again. Some guilt is actually a good thing. It's a sign of a well-developed conscience. However, after it gets our attention and we make the decision to adjust our behavior or thinking in the future, it is best that we get rid of the guilt.

At its extreme, guilt can be debilitating because it is all consuming and self-centering. When you feel guilty, you tend to focus all of your attention on yourself, but not in a good way. The emphasis is on how terrible and awful you are as a person and on how you should be punished and treated with disdain by others. Along with leading to a good deal of suffering, such thoughts are also unproductive. Very often, those who are consumed by guilt are only able to focus on how badly they feel and have difficulty paying attention to why they feel guilty. When we experience such negative emotions, we are prevented from making changes that would eliminate the source of our guilt. When looked at from that perspective, we can understand that guilt inhibits our ability to manage our lives and make them better.

HUMAN BEINGS HAVE SOME POWER OVER THEMSELVES AND THEIR LIVES

Since human beings have the ability to think, plan, and choose, they have some power over their lives. However, the operative word in that statement is *some*. The reality is there are many ways in which our power may be quite limited, and many of the things that directly affect our lives are beyond our control. We can't control the weather, governments, politics, the stock market, and, as we have already mentioned, the people around us. Knowing the limitations of our control is an important part of achieving psychological well-being, also known as happiness.

It's certainly easy enough to pay lip service to this point, because, after all, it's entirely reasonable. Yet there are occasions where we might abandon this basic rule of living. In some situations many of us might waste valuable time, effort, and resources trying to get control over the uncontrollable. We might allow ourselves to become impatient and frustrated because things that are actually beyond our control are not cooperating with our desires. For instance, people who rant and rave while sitting in traffic only manage to ruin their mood and raise their blood pressure, not to mention increasing the stress level of those riding along with them. In certain situations, some may let their frustration build up until they find themselves falling into depression, ill-health, or a chronic state of unhappiness and despair. As one of its major negative side effects, spending time and effort trying to change things that we can't may sometimes cause us to experience emotions that interfere with our thinking processes. As a result, we might miss opportunities to focus on things that we can control and which can improve how we react to uncontrollable events.

This idea is nicely summarized in the serenity prayer, which is attributed to Reinhold Niebuhr and is the motto of Alcoholics Anonymous: *God grant me the serenity to accept the things that I cannot change, courage to change the things I can, and the wisdom to know the difference.* The wisdom to know the difference between what you can control and what you can't is not always readily available. For many of us, wisdom comes slowly. It takes much trial and error and pain and, for some situations, only comes with age. Don't be surprised or disappointed in yourself if you find that you may require a lifetime to develop this wisdom. If you work at it, though, you will ultimately help yourself more than if you give up or keep trying to do the impossible.

Along with certain events and situations, an important truth to recognize is that we can't control other people. Many people have gotten into trouble, and some have driven themselves into depression and anxiety, trying to control others. We might believe that things would go much more smoothly in our lives if people would just do things the way we want them to. After all, don't we know what is best? The truth is we probably don't. However, even if we do know what is best, it is not likely that other people will see it our way. We have little hope of controlling them and getting them to do exactly what we want them to do all of the time.

This is not to say that you can't influence other people with your words and actions. Influencing someone means that we present the other person with information that can help them understand an issue better, and then they can arrive at a conclusion that serves them better. Using the information we provide for them, along with other information, they can make a more informed decision as to what they should do. However, influence is not the same as control. Controlling someone means that we make the decision about what is to be done and the other person does what we tell them to do without making choices on their own.

Suppose your spouse or friend smokes and you believe that they should not do this. You can try to influence them by expressing your concern about their smoking and even do things to help them give up the habit. However, short of locking the smoker in a room, you cannot force that person to quit. In fact, all of the lectures, advice, hints, and even threats will not necessarily cause them to stop smoking. That is a decision they have to make personally, and it is one that they have to own themselves.

Still, trying to control others is a mistake we can occasionally make. Maybe we won't try to control the lives of everyone we know, but we might try with some people, or we might try in some situations. Unfortunately, sometimes we are successful. It is actually more frustrating when we have partial success in getting people to follow our direction. It gives us the false hope that we can control others all or most of the time.

The false belief that we can control others can have damaging consequences. Take, for example, the case of people who marry with the expectation of being able to change their partners. They are not happy with the person they married but hold the belief that, with the right amount of effort and time, they can make that person into someone they would like more. This is a major and an unfortunate mistake that can be torturous and destructive to a marriage. Typically the spouse who wants the other to change continues to be disappointed, while the one who has pressure to be a different person will likely find their marriage to be stressful. The point is that you can help a person develop and change as long as they direct the change, but you can't change a person unless they want to change. As the silly old joke goes, how many psychologists does it take to change a light bulb? Only one, but that's only if the light bulb really wants to change.

Besides, even if it were possible (and it's not), trying to control others does not really help you, and might even suggest you have a few issues of your own to work out. When you try to control another person, you are unconsciously deciding you know the best way for that person to live. The truth is that we all have flaws, and our way of thinking or acting might not in fact be the best way, especially for another person. Secondly, while we may believe that we have other people's best interests at heart when we want them to change, we really don't. We are working from our own interests, and we want them to live and act in a certain way because it fills our own needs, not theirs. Finally, if you try to get someone to act a certain way, you become responsible for the outcomes they experience. That's a responsibility you should be happy to avoid, because when things don't go according to plan, you also end up sharing their problems and getting the blame.

When it comes to other people, you must accept the reality that what you see is what you get. If they have traits that you don't like, you are left with the choice of either accepting them with their faults and keeping them in your life, or breaking off your relationship with them. Turning them into something different is not an option. Acknowledging this fact may lead you away from trying to change them, and that can help you avoid disappointments and frustrations. Coming to terms with this reality is actually a good thing. It takes quite a bit of pressure off you to fix other people's lives and lets you have more time for fixing your own. Keep in mind that trying to change other people is like banging your head against the wall. The best thing about it is that it feels so good when you stop.

SUMMARY

Human beings are a special species, distinct from all others. Our distinctiveness derives from our cognitive functioning, that is, our ability to think and plan. Thinking and planning skills are linked to freedom of choice. While freedom to choose our own path has benefits, it comes at a price. We are responsible for our emotions and behavior, and for the outcomes of our choices. Freedom of choice also gives us some personal control over our lives, but that power is limited to ourselves and our surroundings. Above all, people cannot control others, and trying to do so will create problems for themselves and their relationships.

People have true control over their lives only if they take the time to understand what they can do, accept the responsibilities and consequences of their choices, and make the best choice that they can, given their self-limitations and the limitations of the circumstances in which they find themselves.

2

THE FOUR PSYCHOLOGICAL FUNCTIONS

An understanding as to how our minds work is also essential to understanding yourself. It is generally acknowledged that human beings have four basic psychological functions: perception, cognition, emotion, and behavior. These functions are the tools we use for coping and interacting with the elements that make up our environment, including people, situations, and events.

As an important point, these psychological functions don't work independently of each other. Rather, they work together and affect each other. For example, if we see a person we know, we might react with a thought or emotion, and that in turn could trigger a behavior. If we like the person, we could experience positive feelings and pleasant thoughts. These thoughts and feelings might then lead us to walk up to that person to chat or just shake their hand and say hello. We discuss each of these functions in some detail below to explain their basic elements and how they interact with each other to help us interpret and react to our environment.

PERCEPTION

Perception can be looked at as our information gathering function. People continually take in information from their environment through all of their senses; they hear, see, smell, touch and taste. However, we do not only take in information from our environment in its raw form;

we process it. We change and transform many aspects of the information we receive. Without being aware of it, our perceptional skills convert this information so that it is more in line with our personal experiences, motivations, and expectations.

Said another way, we very often hear and see what we want and expect to hear and see. It has been suggested that the eye is like a camera; that is, many of the anatomical parts of the eye (lens, retina, etc.) have analogous parts in a camera. But in reality, the human eye functions very differently from a camera. It doesn't work alone, but instead is only part of a system that includes the brain. Information comes into the eye and is sent to the brain where it is interpreted and comprehended. What we then comprehend is often a result of the interaction of the information our eyes pick up with the information that is already stored in our brains.

If you have ever been on a diet you probably remember how the whole world seemed to become full of food. You never before noticed so many food commercials on television and how many daily activities are associated with food. This happens because your motivation (hunger and feeling deprived) *tunes* your perceptual system so that you are more keenly aware of the food and food messages around you. You are picking up more messages about food because your brain is focusing on the thing you are missing most. As an act of self-preservation, your brain is keeping you on the lookout for something to eat.

We also use our memories to guide the way we perceive and interpret information taken in by our senses. In an effort to make our environment familiar and understandable, our brains will force-fit what we see into what we already know. In other words, we see what we expect to see and what we are used to seeing. A colleague passed on a story of a teacher who gave a multiple choice test to his class. When the students came into the classroom the teacher had written the answers to the test on the blackboard. After the test was finished, he collected the exams and asked the students if they had noticed that the answers were on the blackboard. Several of the students said that they saw the answers on the board but figured it must be a trick because they had never had the experience of a teacher putting the answers on the blackboard when they took a test. They were unable to interpret the situation accurately because their prior experiences and memories locked them into a specific way of thinking.

Our ability to perceive events in our environment is also affected by our motivation levels. Those of us who have children can attest to the ability to *hear* our children under conditions when we might normally ignore most other sounds in our environment. We know of a man whose wife claimed that he was such a sound sleeper that he could not be awakened by a nuclear attack. While he agreed that this might be so, both he and his wife can also recall many times when he was *violently* awakened at night by one of his son's very faint cries of distress. He was highly motivated to care for and protect his son, so his senses were tuned in to any signs that his child was in distress.

This *tuning* of perception has some very positive benefits. For instance, we can interpret events very quickly because we think we know what we're looking for. That means we can also respond quickly to these events. However, there are times when perceptual tuning can have negative consequences, such as when we face new situations or ones we prefer to avoid, or someone we know behaves in ways we consider out of character. If something happens that is not what we expect or want, we can misinterpret signs or not pay enough attention to specific cues that are important. In marriage counseling, many husbands and wives have stated that they have said certain things many times but their spouses just don't get it. In such instances it may be the case that they just don't want to get it because the message would be too burdensome or unpleasant. Perceptual *tuning* can cause us to miss important things because they fall outside our experiences or are not particularly acceptable to us.

There is a particularly special relationship between emotions and perception. Negative emotions such as anger and anxiety *narrow* perception and prevent us from taking in all of the information available in our environment. It is well documented that test anxiety, defined as feelings of extreme distress often tied to a fear of failing, has a particularly deleterious effect on test performance because it interferes with concentration, reading, and comprehension. This narrowing effect makes it difficult to process information effectively and often has a very negative effect on communication. That is why it is better not to try to solve problems or engage in any very difficult task when you are highly emotionally aroused.

COGNITION

Cognition, or thinking, is a complex set of processes that include memory, problem solving, and creativity. We are thinking virtually all the time, and very often our thoughts are experienced as internal speech. They are internal representations and verbalizations of both our internal and external experiences. The study of the thinking process often emphasizes logic and logical systems. There is much written about the nature of human thinking that will not be reviewed here. Instead, our focus is on understanding the various ways we think and how thought patterns are related to self-awareness and coping with our environment.

Thinking is a very important part of the human experience. It is the basis for understanding ourselves and other people. Most of us feel we really know someone when we have a good idea about how they think. Cognitive processes are also the primary drivers of human behavior. Before we do something, a thought pops up in our minds for us to perform that action.

Thoughts often occur in response to something in our environment. We see or hear something and that causes us to think about that event. Thinking about these events is the means by which we attempt to come to terms with our world and deal with the issues of life. We can solve problems that face us because we have internalized experiences that we can translate into thoughts. We use these thoughts to analyze the issues at hand and choose alternative courses of action.

Our thoughts are greatly affected by our psychological makeup. For example, the directions our thoughts take can be determined by our beliefs. These are the principles that we accept as truths about how the world and other people operate. If we hold firm religious beliefs, we might interpret and think about a particular situation as God's work. If we believe in predestination, we might use fatalistic thoughts, such as karma, as a way to explain situations to ourselves. If we win at a casino, we might think it's our lucky day—if we believe in such things as luck. People have many beliefs and it can be argued that our system of beliefs is what makes us unique from other people.

BELIEFS

Beliefs are complex processes that are personally indicative and personally predictive. That is, they imply important attributes about us and predict what will happen to us. If I hold the belief that *I am ugly*, this implies something negative about me and says something about what will happen to me in my relationships with others. Beliefs are also an essential part of how we deal with other people. For example, if you know your friend holds conservative beliefs on politics, you have a pretty good idea how they would react to a new social policy. Because they reveal so much about us and affect how we think, act, and feel, beliefs occupy a critical role in understanding ourselves.

Rational and Irrational Beliefs

A very prominent humanistic psychologist, Dr. Albert Ellis, has postulated the existence of two kinds of beliefs, rational and irrational. Rational beliefs are those that (1) conform to the rules of logic, (2) are consistent with our general experience, and (3) are consistent with our personal goals. Irrational beliefs are those that violate any one of these rules, that is, do not conform to the rules of logic, are not consistent with general experience, and are not consistent with our goals.

If we hold the belief that all human beings make mistakes, we hold a rational belief. It is rational because it is logical, given what we know about human behavior. It is consistent with our experiences both with others and with ourselves, because we have found that we and other people make mistakes. It is also consistent with our goals because once we acknowledge that we make mistakes, we allow ourselves the opportunity to dedicate both time and resources to deal with our mistakes.

On the other hand, if we hold the belief that human beings should never make a mistake, we hold an irrational belief. It is irrational because it is illogical if one understands human nature. It is inconsistent with our experiences because we all make mistakes and have witnessed others doing the same thing. It also interferes with us attaining our goals because it prevents us from planning for mistakes and causes us to upset ourselves when mistakes happen.

As Dr. Ellis has pointed out, all human beings hold both rational and irrational beliefs. In fact, irrational thinking is as much a part of human nature as is rational thinking. As a general rule, we like to think of ourselves as being totally rational all the time. So we may find it difficult to accept the fact that part of the nature of our thinking processes is to, at times, think irrationally. In fact, we can hold both irrational and rational beliefs about the same issue and at the same time, even if they appear to contradict each other. Irrational beliefs are part of everyone's thinking even though we may not always recognize that we hold them. It's part of being human, which is to say, imperfect.

Here's an example that illustrates simultaneous rational and irrational thinking. If you ask most people if they expect that every person with whom they interact will like and admire them, they would probably say no. They would probably say that they believe that it is likely that only a proportion of those people with whom they have contact will like and admire them. They probably realize that some people may dislike them for reasons that have little to do with their personal characteristics. For example, they may bear a physical resemblance to a disliked ex-boyfriend, abusive father, or an unfriendly boss. Or other people may just be having a bad day and don't feel good about anyone at the moment.

Now, imagine you are at a party with a hundred other guests. At this party, all of the guests decide to give you their evaluation of you. One by one each person at the party approaches you and heaps large doses of praise and adulation on you. Ninety-nine of the guests tell you that you are physically attractive, intelligent, creative, kind, and trustworthy and you possess every other positive characteristic any person would want to have. However, the hundredth person takes a different perspective. He or she is just not that taken with you. In that person's book, you are *just okay,* but nobody special and he or she would not go out of their way to spend time with you.

How do you imagine most people would think about what this last guest said? They probably would spend a good deal of time wondering why that hundredth person did not give them the same level of adulation and praise that the others did. They might come to the conclusion that if everyone else loved them, then there must be something wrong with this person if he or she didn't feel the same way, or there might be something wrong with themselves.

The point here is that even though we hold the rational belief that no one can be loved by everyone, we can also hold the irrational belief that everyone must approve and admire you at all times. If we did not hold this belief, we would be completely accepting of the judgment of that hundredth person. If you were a baseball player and batted .990 (99/100), you would hold every record in hitting. In other words, you wouldn't be perfect, but not being perfect would still be extremely good, but sometimes we might not be able to see it that way.

From our perspective, most people also hold the irrational belief that they should never make a mistake. Your initial reaction to this statement might be that this is not the case. However, if it were not true, people would never get as upset and disturbed as they do by the mistakes they make. While there may be times when we can accept our mistakes and move on, sometimes we can't. Try to remember how upset you were and how long you were upset the last time you discovered you made a mistake over something that was important to you. If you didn't believe you should not make mistakes, you would be more forgiving of yourself and not have gotten upset. You might also have moved more quickly to correct your mistake because you weren't blocked by how bad you were feeling.

The Consequences of Irrational Beliefs

As we alluded to in the above, irrational thinking always has very negative consequences. It creates negative emotional states, such as anxiety or depression, which negatively affect other aspects of human functioning, such as our physical and mental health. Irrational thinking is also negative in that it prevents us from taking positive action to deal with the problems that face us. When we make a mistake we often spend more time concentrating on the mistake and the emotions that result than we do on correcting the mistake.

There was once a researcher who had a student working for him whose work was usually of the highest caliber. While working on an important project, this student made some clerical errors. As a result, the researcher found himself in a potentially embarrassing position, and several of the tasks had to be redone. Upon discovering the errors, the student became agitated to the point of distraction. His reaction was in spite of the fact that the researcher was not upset and expressed that to the student. After some time the student asked the researcher in a frantic tone what could possibly be done to make up for the mistakes he had made. The researcher calmly told him that he should fix the mistakes and be sure to double-check his work in the future. These two obvious solutions were not so obvious to the student because he spent too much time beating himself up.

Our point here is that irrationality *freezes* us. Such beliefs as described above often cause us to focus on ourselves and the emotions that we're experiencing, rather than the event itself. Because we can become distracted, these emotions often prevent us from finding solutions to our problems. Other irrational beliefs, such as prejudice or the idea that we can control another person, block us from seeing the world as it really is and can lead to close-mindedness. If we cannot see things accurately, it's hard to make correct decisions. It is like putting our feet into hardening cement; the longer we stay there, the less likely we will be to move out of it. It is for this reason that we need to develop an awareness of our irrational thoughts and spend some time disabusing ourselves of them. Being aware of our irrational beliefs gives us a better way of understanding what we can change and what is beyond our control.

Of course, we must accept the fact that we will always hold onto many irrational beliefs. However, we can become more aware of them. Additionally, we can fight against those irrational beliefs that are particularly troublesome by countering with more rational ones. If you find yourself upset over making a mistake, have a conversation with yourself. Tell yourself that you are being irrational and that dwelling on your mistake is not helping. Don't put yourself down for thinking irrationally. Accept yourself as human, and accept that you will make mistakes.

Accepting that you will make mistakes is important, but you must also put in the effort to learn from your mistakes. Acceptance only makes it easier for you to identify a problem. While this is a critical step if learning or changing is to occur, it's only part of the issue. We also have to come up with solutions to fix a problem. Even if you're faced with a mistake that can't be changed or fixed, you can still try to do better in the future. Doing better means you take steps to change how you approach an issue so that you are most likely not to repeat the same mistakes.

What Makes a Belief Irrational?

There are many irrational beliefs that are held by most of us. Of course, any list would not be exhaustive since many irrational ideas are specific to individuals, because we each have a different set of experiences from which they're derived. Nevertheless, many years ago, Albert Ellis compiled an extensive list of the most commonly encountered irrational beliefs. Three of these that are particularly germane to our topic are listed below. Each of these beliefs is irrational because it cannot be proven, does not fit with our experience, and will be counterproductive to solving a problem:

1. We must have the love and approval of everyone we find significant.
2. We must be thoroughly competent and successful at everything we do.
3. When people treat us unfairly, we should blame and damn them and see them as evil, wicked, and rotten.

One of the key ingredients that make beliefs irrational is the component of *absoluteness*. Irrational beliefs often contain the words *should* and *must* and imply a demand about the world and the people in it. Absolutes by definition imply that a situation or event will occur repeatedly in the same way, regardless of whether or not there are interceding conditions. Absolutes can never fit human behavior because people are fallible and have limited abilities, and thus cannot perform exactly the same way all the time. Also, we cannot apply absolute rules to events in the world because these events are largely out of the control of individuals. Even if we have *some* control over *some* of the events in the world, that control is very limited. This is true whether you are a president of a country or a factory worker.

When we think of people and our environment in terms of absolutes, we tend to make demands that people and events repeatedly behave just as we want them to. Unfortunately, all of the demanding in the world will not get us what we want. Our demands will not change the fact that people operate in their own self-interest and the world has the quality of randomness to it. In fact, making demands on others will decrease the likelihood that you will get what you want. Excessive demands are a turnoff. People are usually reluctant to be cooperative and helpful to those who are demanding because they find them difficult to deal with. Consequently, because demands usually are an indication that we have a problem with someone, their reluctance to cooperate means we won't be effective in solving that problem.

We are not saying there are no absolutes at all. There are laws of physics, for example, that don't vary. As might be suggested from the work of Isaac Newton, in the absence of something blocking its path, an apple that falls from a tree will *always* make its way to the ground. But the laws of physics do not apply to people. With rare exceptions, we cannot apply absolutes to any description or expectation about human beings and human behavior. Religious standards such as the Ten Commandments, which are phrased in absolute terms (Thou Shalt Not), wouldn't need to exist if we thought that human beings wouldn't occasionally engage in behaviors that are contrary to them.

That's not to say that absolutes have no role at all when it comes to people. They can serve us as a standard of excellence or as goals toward which we aspire. However, they cannot serve as descriptions or expectations of what is likely to happen. For example, it is desirable to aspire never to lie, but to expect or demand that human beings will never lie is irrational and can lead to disappointment, frustration, and anger. Our point here is that we don't want you to lower your standards for your behavior; we just want you to set them realistically so that you will upset yourself less when the world does not go as you want it to.

EMOTIONS

Emotions may be the most complicated of all psychological functions. There are a number of theories from a variety of disciplines as to what exactly occurs when we experience an emotion, including psychology, sociology, psychophysiology, and neurology, to name a few. For our purposes, a good way to think about emotions is that they are changes in normal or usual functioning, typically as a positive or negative reaction to events that are occurring in our environment or in our own heads. They are highly subjective and we are aware that we have experienced an emotional reaction. They are also intertwined with our thoughts and can motivate us to do or say something.

As familiar as we are with our emotions, they really defy explanation. It is difficult to describe what it's actually like to experience an emotion. Very often we are only able to communicate about emotions by giving them a label or name. Take, for example, the experience of anger. We can talk about the thoughts associated with anger (*you cheated on me, I am hurt*). You can describe the physical experiences associated with being angry (pains in the stomach, headaches, tightness in the chest, seeing red). However, such descriptions do not capture the entire experience of anger; they only convey the outward expressions of it.

While it seems the best we can do is to label emotions, we may not always label them accurately. This is particularly true when there is some social censure about particular emotions. For example, people often report that they are disappointed, hurt, or annoyed, when really they are angry. Anger is one of those emotions that can be viewed negatively in this society. We tend to associate anger with loss of control, aggression, violence, and being *bad*. Consequently, many people would prefer to label how they are feeling as something other than anger. They might believe that there is something wrong with them, or they may believe they will be judged negatively by others, if they claim to be angry.

A colleague passed on a story about a couple he was seeing in marriage counseling. During many of the sessions, the wife would often insist that the husband answer her questions immediately. She would repeatedly ask him to explain his behavior or wanted to know why he doesn't listen to her. If he was not immediately forthcoming she would repeat her questions over and over again. Each time she did so, he would withdraw from the interaction and refuse to talk. She would then become more aggressive about her questioning and he would then withdraw further.

During one session the therapist noticed that the husband appeared to become very angry when this cycle happened. The therapist said to him that he appeared to be angry. The husband shouted, *I am not angry, why do you accuse me of being angry? I'm just a little annoyed!* The therapist then asked him why it would be so bad if he were angry. This led to a long discussion about experiencing and expressing anger. The husband mentioned that feeling anger is inappropriate, and he would prefer not to express himself when he felt that way. The therapist pointed out how his approach helped prolong the negative interaction with his wife. Failing to recognize and deal with his anger was preventing him from making progress in trying to change the dysfunctional communication styles between him and his wife. This discussion also helped the wife to see exactly how she was also contributing to the negative interaction and led to further conversations about methods they could use to facilitate more productive communication.

Although we may not be able to define or explain our emotions fully, we are able to talk about them. When we talk about our emotions, we often will discover much about the way we think. That's because there is a very strong connection between emotions and thoughts. Both thoughts and emotions can feed on each other. A positive or negative emotion can trigger thoughts that are consistent with that emotion. Take, for example, a situation where someone you know has disappointed you. You will probably experience that disappointment as a negative emotion. That negative emotion might then lead you to think about all the other times this person has disappointed you in the past, that is, you will experience negative thoughts.

The above situation can also happen in reverse. Positive and negative thoughts can also be the catalyst for emotions. If you have a negative thought about someone, you can experience a corresponding negative emotion about that person. If you think that someone is treating you with disrespect, that thought will lead you to be upset or angry. Your anger might then lead you to think about characteristics about this person that you don't like, and that can fuel your anger. When that type of situation takes place, we are actually getting caught up in a cycle of negativity, with a negative thought producing a negative emotion, which then produces another negative thought, followed by another negative emotion, and so on. Such patterns can have a negative impact on our overall psychological well-being.

People are sometimes reluctant to talk about their negative emotions because they are part of the unpleasant and frustrating events we have experienced. Nevertheless, talking to ourselves about negative emotions is a good way to uncover our irrational beliefs. This self-talk will help us dispute these beliefs and decrease the misery and unhappiness they can cause. On the other hand, avoiding the examination of negative emotions will prevent us from solving the problems in our lives and can contribute to our unhappiness. We all need to spend time exploring and talking about our emotions. Such activity will help us know ourselves better and ultimately improve our lives.

BEHAVIOR

When we talk about behavior we refer to any action in which human beings engage. We walk, talk, work at our jobs, eat, cry, smile, and many other things. Any human action that can be observed can be considered to be a behavior. It can be simple (movement of a finger) or complex (solve a difficult problem). We could, as behaviorists do, also consider thinking and emoting as behaviors because these are actions that we can observe personally, even though they may not be observable to others. However, we prefer to consider thoughts and emotions separately because they have a central role in controlling our behaviors that are directly observable by others, such as our actions or words.

Behaviors are important in relationships, because they provide feedback about how we feel or how we have interpreted something said or done by another person. If someone does something nice for us, we will likely be very pleased and grateful. If we only *think* about how grateful and pleased we are, no one else, especially the person who did something nice for us, will know how we are reacting. In fact, the failure to say or do anything that indicates that we are pleased and grateful might be interpreted by the other person that we are not. It is important to distinguish between what we feel (emotions), what we think (cognitions), and what we do (behaviors). The last of these is the only way that others truly understand you and what you are thinking. On the other hand, without some form of behavioral expression, people can feel they are not connected to you, and they can easily misinterpret your reactions.

We should note that expressing positive behaviors, either as actions, words, or facial expressions, can go a long way in enhancing your personal relationships. If we take the time to tell our spouse that we are pleased and grateful, he or she can observe this behavior and it will likely have a very positive effect. Our spouse will feel appreciated and valued as an individual. When we show others that we value them, that leads them to feel good about themselves and it also helps them feel good about us. That can lead to stronger emotional bonds between the two of you, and a greater inclination for you and your spouse to be nice to each other.

SUMMARY

Human beings have four essential psychological functions: perception, cognition, emotion, and behavior. These functions interact with and affect each other, and work together to guide us in how we interact with our environment and other people. The most important human function is cognition because it includes our beliefs, and these influence all other functions. To understand the essence of any individual is to understand her or his beliefs. In the following chapter we discuss how our emotions and thoughts are controlled by our beliefs and how beliefs are related to the concepts of conscious and unconscious functioning.

3

BELIEFS, EMOTIONS, CONSCIOUS AND UNCONSCIOUS FUNCTIONING

Psychological well-being and effective living requires that we have a full understanding of the source and adaptability of our emotions. As we pointed out in the previous chapter, our beliefs are the driving force behind our thoughts, emotions, and behaviors. In that sense, they establish the tone for how we interact with our environment and play an important role in defining the quality of our relationships with other people.

In this chapter we explore the relationship between our belief systems and the resulting emotions. Our goal is to explain how our beliefs can affect the ways we interpret situations and events in our lives and the kinds of emotions that we associate with these situations and events. We also look at two different types of thought processes, conscious and unconscious. We will illustrate the roles played by each of these cognitive functions with respect to the types of beliefs we hold and the emotions we experience. We then relate all of these concepts to our understanding of human functioning.

THE RELATIONSHIP BETWEEN BELIEFS AND EMOTIONS

Dr. Albert Ellis provided strong evidence that there is a causal relationship between beliefs and emotions. Simply put, he said that beliefs cause emotions. It's not always easy to recognize or understand the causal relationship because we tend to think that our emotions spring directly from something that has happened to us. If we ask a person who is angry why she is angry, she is likely to claim that the cause of her anger is some event or other person.

Take the example of a husband and wife who are in the middle of a conflict. A wife states that she is angry because her husband yelled at her. Essentially, she is saying that her husband's yelling is the outside or activating event (A: activator) that caused her emotion of anger (C: consequence). If this were true, then she should be angry every time her husband yelled at her. Also, if her spouse did not yell at her, then her anger should greatly decrease or disappear. Neither of these things is likely to be true all the time. There might be times when his yelling is seen by him as justified, such as if she yelled at him first. While yelling on both sides is certainly inappropriate, she is not likely to claim she is angry if his yelling occurred in response to hers. Rather, we would argue that there is something that exists between his yelling and her anger. It seems more reasonable to assume that his yelling was an activating event (A) that triggered an irrational belief (B) (he should never yell at me) which caused the consequence (C) of her feeling angry.

As another example, suppose a professor gives three male students a grade of B for a course. Also, suppose that upon receiving the grade the first student becomes elated, the second student becomes depressed and agitated, and the third student is indifferent. Can we say that the activating event of getting a B caused the three different emotions? If this were true, the reactions of the three students should be similar. Since they are different, it suggests that something else was going on.

If we postulate that the three different emotions were caused by three different beliefs, the situation becomes understandable. The student who was elated may have been hoping but not expecting to get a B. He was elated because he got a grade that he considered to be optimum for him under the prevailing circumstances. This grade symbolized a high level of success and achievement for that student. The student who became depressed and agitated probably expected an A. This student most likely thought of himself as failing by getting less than an A. The student who was indifferent probably saw grades as unimportant to him or his life and therefore did not have a strong emotional reaction in either direction for the grade he was given.

In both of the above examples, it is readily apparent that it is not the activating events (A), the yelling or the grade, that caused the consequences of emotions and behaviors (C). Instead, it was a result of each person's beliefs (B). Dr. Ellis referred to this as the ABCs of human adjustment. His central idea can be summarized as follows: *it's not the events of the world that cause our emotions; it is the meaning that we attach to those events.*

Dr. Ellis also stated that there are two kinds of emotions, appropriate and inappropriate. We prefer to call the two types *adaptive* and *nonadaptive* because those labels take into account how each type of emotion affects our day-to-day living. Emotions such as depression, anxiety, and anger are considered to be nonadaptive because they disrupt us physically and they prevent us from making improvements in our lives. Nonadaptive emotions are the ones that freeze us into inactivity. They cause us to dwell on our feelings rather than work on the issues that are the cause of these feelings. We might experience a sense of helplessness about our situation when nonadaptive emotions dominate our thought patterns and that can make us feel we have no control over our lives.

Adaptive emotions, such as love, happiness, sadness, concern, and annoyance enrich our lives in that they add to and broaden our experiences. They are in effect the *spice* of life. Such emotions as happiness or sadness focus our thinking to the sources of these feelings. When we feel sad because a loved one dies, we tend to think about that person: the positive experiences from the past or how much we enjoyed that person. When we're in love, our thoughts are preoccupied with the target of our affections. The point here is that adaptive emotions lead us to focus on the events in our lives and absorb us into the world.

The different types of emotions we experience are linked to the different types of beliefs we discussed in the previous chapter. Nonadaptive emotions are caused by irrational beliefs and adaptive emotions are caused by rational beliefs. If we feel anxious or depressed over the loss of a loved one, our thoughts tend to be preoccupied with how miserable we feel. We're focusing on ourselves, possibly thinking we can't live without that person. The irrational belief that may be working in this case is that *I* can't live without that person, with the emphasis on *I*. However, the truth is, even though we feel sad, which is normal and to be expected, we will go on living. Nonadaptive emotions cause us to focus inward and away from the world, making us feel isolated and helpless. That's their freezing effect. When we're focused inward, we're not focusing on our problems and our emotions, and that means we can't move forward or come up with solutions to those problems.

Because nonadaptive emotions are driven by irrational beliefs, we can use them as a way of identifying our irrational beliefs. If you feel angry, you can focus your attention on trying to discover the irrational belief that is causing you to feel that way. This idea is important because it's not always easy to identify irrational beliefs without some clues to help us get there. As we mentioned in the previous chapter, irrational beliefs can be operating in our minds at the same time as our rational beliefs. When they're operating side by side, it can be difficult to figure out which beliefs are driving which emotions. We might think that we feel a particular way because of a rational belief. However, if we know the emotion we're experiencing is nonadaptive, then you also know that it is springing from an irrational belief. In other words, we can use the emotions we're feeling as an indicator or sign as to what type of beliefs are occupying our minds. In that way we can identify them more clearly and then work on ways to decrease their influence on our thoughts, feelings, and actions.

CONSCIOUS AND UNCONSCIOUS FUNCTIONING

The idea that human cognitive processes can be divided into conscious and unconscious (nonaware) parts has existed for a long time. In fact, psychologists have had an ongoing debate over the past hundred or so years as to the nature of unconscious processes. Freud postulated that the unconscious mind contains the majority of human thought process-es. One of the most significant principles for Freud had to do with the manner in which conscious processes are pushed into the unconscious. He believed that threatening or unwanted thoughts are *repressed* or forced into the unconscious mind. That takes place as a way of protect-ing ourselves. Because we are not consciously aware of such negative thoughts when they are repressed, they're less likely to make us feel anxious.

While the thoughts that occur at an unconscious level are never observed or recognized directly, they still exert a good deal of influence indirectly into everyday cognitive functioning. For Freud, unconscious thoughts exist in symbolic form in our minds, and can only be understood by interpreting the symbols in terms of their underlying unconscious meaning. For example, if a young child is traumatized by having been bitten by a white dog, he may manifest that trauma as an extreme fear of Santa Claus. In this situation, the whiteness of the dog becomes associated with a salient aspect of Santa Claus, his white beard. Therefore, for Freud and his followers, much of the therapeutic process involves analyzing or interpreting the meaning of manifest thoughts and behaviors to uncover their underlying or unconscious meaning.

Freud saw *repression* as the most important process or defense because it protects us from being overwhelmed by anxiety and as a result being locked into a state of dysfunction. He believed that repression is related to survival and that it takes a great deal of time and effort to break through the force of repression and make us aware of our unconscious thoughts. This explains why psychoanalysis, Freud's therapeutic system, takes so long and is so difficult to complete.

Although we do not adhere to all of Freud's ideas, we and many other professionals in the field of psychology recognize the value of many of them. There certainly is validity to the idea that there is an unconscious level of human functioning that operates on principles different from those of conscious functioning. We do not, however, necessarily think that we can only become aware of our unconscious thoughts through a long, drawn-out process in which one spends many years on an analyst's couch. Instead, we believe that intense and relatively frequent self-reflection can help us reach and understand our unconscious processes.

CONSCIOUS-RATIONAL THINKING

Much of human thinking that takes place is conscious. These are the thoughts that we are aware of and say to ourselves. Conscious thinking is rational. By that we mean it follows the rules of logic and can be analyzed and understood. It is influenced by the concepts of time and space and we are able to make a clear distinction between the past, present, and future. It is also influenced by our previous experiences, motivations, and expectations. We use conscious-rational thinking to solve problems, plan for the future, and cope with our day-to-day needs and challenges.

Since conscious thinking is rational, it makes sense that our rational beliefs are also found at the conscious level. Because conscious thinking tends to be logical, we can use it to tell if our beliefs are rational or irrational. When we consciously become aware of our irrational thoughts we can often clearly see the basis for their irrationality. This is not to say that we can easily change them, but we usually have the ability to recognize them for what they are. At times we might find ourselves saying that we feel or believe something, and while we know that it's irrational to think that way, we just can't help it. In other words, we can see the irrationality of our thinking, but we have trouble changing our beliefs. Learning to differentiate between rational and irrational beliefs is an important step. From there we have an idea of what thinking patterns we need to work on to develop more useful and effective belief systems.

UNCONSCIOUS-IRRATIONAL THINKING

As we've mentioned, unconscious functioning is where information lies about which we have no awareness. However, unlike the Freudian idea of unconscious, in which unpleasant thoughts are believed to be repressed, we postulate that much of this information (thoughts, memories, and beliefs) may have never been in consciousness. Rather, we suggest that much of the information we have learned from the early stages of our lives is stored unconsciously, but that information is not necessarily under the force of *repression*. In other words, this information has not been placed deep into our memories as a way of protecting ourselves, but instead is just stored there along with a variety of other experiences. Looked at in another way, if all the information we have accumulated over the years was always present in our consciousness, we'd be overloaded with information inserting itself into our thoughts, and that would make it difficult to focus on issues that are important at any one point in time. Therefore, it's important for our day-to-day functioning that we have the information we need right now to be conscious, and the rest to be stored unconsciously.

There are actually a few ways information gets into our unconscious. For example, the last few decades of research in developmental psychology have demonstrated that infants learn much more than we previously thought. Psychologists have discovered that, from the moment of birth (and maybe even prenatally), we begin learning and are affected by our environment, although we are not necessarily aware that we are learning. We process information on many different levels and for some of this information we may not consciously intend to and/ or are unaware that we are processing it. Such ways of accumulating information are referred to as incidental learning and have been demonstrated to exist in human beings, but also in a number of other animal species.

As adults we continue to learn incidentally. Each of us has had the experience of knowing something without having made a concerted effort to learn that information intentionally. Information that we have learned incidentally may be stored unconsciously, but it's not necessarily repressed. In fact, unconscious information will move in and out of consciousness, usually because an outside event or another conscious thought will serve as a trigger. All of us have had the experience of a thought entering our minds and we're left wondering why we just had that thought or memory.

Of course, we don't deny the existence of repression completely, especially when it comes to unpleasant or threatening thoughts. Blocking out negative thoughts happens, but repression is not the only way that information moves in and out of our consciousness. For example it's not uncommon for couples who have been in unhappy marriages for ten or more years to claim that their marriages have lasted that long because they forget most of the unpleasant things that have happened over the years. However, those same couples will also have other unconscious memories about their marriages that are pleasant and not necessarily threatening.

The unconscious level of functioning has characteristics that are opposite to those of the conscious level. Unconscious thinking does not follow the rules of logic and reason and is uninfluenced by time. In other words, there is no clear distinction between past, present, and future. Time is irrelevant for unconscious thoughts, because the greatest emphasis is on the here and now. According to Freud, functioning at this level is characterized by an irrational drive to immediately satisfy a need and reduce discomfort.

The unconscious level of functioning is where irrational beliefs reside. The fact that the two types of beliefs, rational and irrational, reside in different levels of human functioning, the conscious and the unconscious, helps us to understand why people can hold both types of beliefs about the same issue at the same time. It also can be used to explain why human thinking and behavior is not always clearly understandable and predictable. For each of us, there will be times when we're thinking rationally, but there will be other times when irrationality and the unconscious, with its illogical and unpredictable nature, will dominate our thoughts and actions.

MENTAL IMAGING

Human beings have active and vivid imaginations. We can conjure up in our minds images that are a representation of the world and events, even though these events are not occurring at the time. Imaging is another form of thinking and can be useful for helping us understand how the world works. Imaging allows us to consider the possibilities that exist in life. We can, for example, use imaging to solve problems. We can imagine the sequence of events that will likely occur from different choices before actually making a final decision. By predicting how events would unfold, we can then make the decision that works out best for us. In the form of daydreaming, it also can be recreational and relaxing.

Some people might hold onto a myth about imagery that prevents them from understanding its usefulness and benefits. The myth stems from confusing imagining or thinking about something as being the same as doing that thing. According to this way of thinking, if you imagine what it would be like to rob a bank, it is the same as actually robbing the bank. This idea is a myth because imagining some action is not the same as doing or intending to do that action. The difference lies in an action of the will (intending) versus an action of the mind (imaging). Responsibility for actions comes from actually doing the action or intending to do the action. This myth can be destructive because it leads people to become afraid of their images, especially those having to do with sex or violence. This fear prevents them from using imaging as a positive tool for exploration and recreation.

Mental images generally come from the conscious level, and are rational. There are, however, some mental images that enter our consciousness from, and are affected by, our unconscious or irrational thoughts. Images of this type seem to come out of the blue and can catch us by surprise. Sometimes they're pleasant, such as when they're about sex. However, others can be unpleasant, such as when they're about rejection or they have aggressive themes. These images can also be quite disturbing because we're not sure where they come from or what negative things they might infer about ourselves.

A patient once reported that he occasionally had images of hurting other people. These images were not very violent or graphic and were very short-lived. He said that he worried a great deal because he thought these images might represent some deep-seated anger. He feared that, at some point, they would break through and he would act on them. When he was told that these occur naturally in people's minds, but they were not commands that he had to obey, he was relieved. As therapy progressed, he reported having fewer of these images and he was no longer disturbed by them. However, if he hadn't brought up the issue during a session, he would have continued to hold onto his assumptions that such images suggested he had emotional problems.

The truth is imaging from either the conscious or unconscious mind represent natural tendencies in human beings and are best regarded as normal manifestations, unless they are so frequent as to be debilitating. If we become afraid of our own images because we see them as unconscious demands that must be obeyed, we will miss a great deal of pleasure in life, and an opportunity to learn something about ourselves. These images give us a chance to explore alternative ways to behave in these situations and therefore allow us to have richer experiences and make more thoughtful choices.

SUMMARY

The relationship between beliefs and emotions is an important one because beliefs are what underlie our emotions. Understanding this relationship allows us to take some control over our emotional life because we can then be empowered to use our emotions in a constructive and positive way.

In trying to understand the relationship between beliefs and emotions, it is necessary to understand the relationship between the two levels of consciousness. The conscious level is the source of rational thinking and rational beliefs, while irrational thinking and beliefs reside in the unconscious. It is a normal part of human nature to have both rational and irrational beliefs, and both can be working at the same time to direct our thinking and behavior.

The dichotomy between conscious and unconscious thinking has been proposed by many psychologists, writers, political theorists, and others who attempt to understand human nature. It can be used to understand the struggle of human existence that is a major theme in all of our lives. It can provide an explanation why, for example, we might find that we hold thoughts that are in conflict with each other.

It is worthwhile to spend time contemplating the struggle between rational and irrational beliefs and to realize that it is as much a part of our nature as any other human characteristic. Your job is to work on recognizing the dichotomy and use your rationality to understand that irrational beliefs are unproductive. The key to better psychological well-being is to try to substitute rational beliefs for irrational ones and thereby decrease nonadaptive emotions and increase adaptive ones.

It is good to keep in mind that we are powerful, thinking, choosing, and responsible living beings. It is necessary to avoid the idea that human beings are passive and controlled by outside forces. Instead, try to adopt the idea that we are more in control of our lives when we take an active role in changing the things we can change and actively accept those that are beyond our control.

4

SOME SPECIFICS ABOUT UNDERSTANDING OURSELVES AND OTHERS

From what we discussed in the previous chapters, it should be apparent that there are quite a few ways that our minds process and use information, which affects our thought patterns. Some ways of thinking are healthy and allow us to understand situations and people in a way that enhances our lives. Other ways of thinking, however, are debilitating; they prevent us from interpreting things so that we can live as well as possible. It may also be obvious that there are a lot of things that you can do on your own to change your thinking patterns so that you can improve your psychological health. In this chapter we cover a few other ideas for you to consider that can move you farther along the path to well-being.

Note that these are not necessarily hard and fast rules. Rather, they are meant to provide some guidance as to ways of thinking and acting that can help you cope better with day-to-day issues and improve the quality of your relationships with other people. Quite a few of these we have discussed in previous chapters, but they are worth repeating, if only to speed you along in the learning process.

- **Take Time for You**

We all recognize the importance of taking time for ourselves for personal hygiene, exercise, and other activities that maintain our physical health. Each of us has probably experienced periods in our lives when our eating habits weren't very healthy or we weren't physically active enough. When these bad habits come to dominate our thoughts, we usually take stock of the situation and get back on track by dieting and working out more.

The same can happen with your emotional well-being. It's just as important to spend some time each day monitoring our psychological health. We might, for example, fall into a pattern of negativity, possibly activated by extended periods of stress or some traumatic event. As we've pointed out, dysfunctional thinking can be habit forming, and it can happen to each of us without our being aware that it has happened. Sometimes it can be difficult to break out of such patterns because we tend to be preoccupied with the hectic business of everyday life, and because negative thoughts and emotions feed on each other, creating an ongoing cycle of negativity.

The best way to avoid falling into a mental rut is through personal vigilance, and the best way to stay vigilant is through introspection. Self-reflection and introspection are the tools we use to think about the events in our lives and review the kinds of emotions and thoughts we experienced during those events. As we do so, our goal is to understand the source of our feelings and try to determine whether we had any episodes when irrational beliefs and inappropriate emotions dominated our thoughts, causing us to think or act in ways that were against our best interests. When we uncover irrationality, we can then focus on coming up with ways to deal with the same situations in a more effective and rational manner in the future.

All psychologists agree that an important thing for living a healthy life is to learn to live *with* yourself—not *by* yourself, but *with* yourself. Make a commitment to take the time each day to spend some time with you. The more you get to know yourself, and the more time you spend examining your own values, thoughts, and beliefs, the better off you will be as a person and the better off all of your various relationships will be.

• Life Requires Continuous Adjusting

We live in a world that is constantly fluctuating and evolving around us. Each day we are challenged with issues and problems that require our attention and energy. Some of these situations are new to us and require us to think or act in new ways. Other times we may be frustrated because problems we believe we have already resolved come up over and over again.

Accepting the reality of an ever-changing world is essential to adjusting. We use the term *adjusting* rather than adjustment to emphasize the point that it is a continuous process of responding to our ever-changing world. When we acknowledge that things constantly change, we open ourselves to the possibility of adjusting our thinking to fit situations as they stand in the present rather than rely on solutions that applied to the past. As an important point, because our world continues to evolve, most solutions to problems are at best temporary, fitting a situation as it occurred under past circumstances and conditions. We may find, for example, that solutions to old problems that worked in the past don't work in the present. At that point it's best to direct our energy to finding new solutions, rather than fall into the trap of becoming upset because the old ones no longer work.

A person once asked a psychologist how he could become perfectly well-adjusted. The psychologist told him that the only permanently well-adjusted people she knew about were in the cemetery. Change is natural and normal in all things, and that includes people. Many of the needs, interests, personal tastes, and values we have as young adults are different from those we had as children, and they're likely to be different again when we get older. Living well requires us to adapt to our environment as it stands right now.

• Acceptance Is Fundamental to Adjusting

As Dr. Ellis has pointed out, *acceptance* is the starting point for greater happiness and less misery. When we say acceptance we mean the recognition of reality. Because it is linked to reality, acknowledging that we live in an ever-fluctuating world is a prerequisite to acceptance. We cannot accept reality until we know what it is. Note that acceptance is different from approval. If we have problems, we can't do much about them until we accept the fact that they exist. Acceptance is also not judgment. It does not mean that you approve, desire, or have any positive feeling toward the thing that you are accepting. It's simply an acknowledgment that something exists.

Lack of acceptance, on the other hand, is essentially the denial of reality. As its most damaging feature, it leaves people unprepared to deal with their problems. Unfortunately, unattended problems usually don't get better by themselves; they usually get much worse. If we want to change our lives and continue our adjusting, accepting reality is the first stage of dealing with our problems.

It is important to point out that acceptance is an *active* process, not a passive one. True acceptance tends to come in stages, and it can require a good deal of effort. Often the things we need to accept are offensive and unpleasant to us, and that makes acceptance of these things difficult. While there will certainly be some things we may never come to completely accept, we can become better at coping with them by dealing with the irrational beliefs that cause us to deny what we need to accept.

True acceptance can also be especially difficult when it comes to situations and events that are beyond our control. As Dr. Ellis has argued, much of the world is uncontrollable and unpredictable, and we are better off not trying to control the things that we can't control. In fact, when we refuse to accept situations we cannot control, such as rejection by someone we love, we will find that we have wasted our time. That's because we're no closer to a solution and as a result no happier. On the other hand, the more we accept the situations we cannot change, the less unhappy we will be with those situations.

• Responsibility Is Not Blame

In the earlier chapters, we have emphasized the importance of taking responsibility for our emotions and behaviors. While we recognize the importance of responsibility, we want to emphasize again the importance of distinguishing between responsibility and blame. Responsibility is the recognition of the connection between what we do and what happens as a result of what we do. When we take responsibility, we acknowledge that we have the power to make those changes in our lives that we have the power to change. There is nothing inherently good or bad about responsibility. We can have good or bad outcomes from our choices, but responsibility in and of itself is simply a rational thinking process in which we understand that we own the outcomes from our choices.

Blame, on the other hand, is a very negative attitude or behavior that can be put on us by others or it can be self-inflicted; it is the root of much human misery. When we blame someone, we imply the need for punishment and retribution. Punishment and retribution solve very little and often germinate all of the negative aspects of human behavior, including aggression, lying, and hate. When we blame ourselves, we experience guilt, and that is a debilitating emotion. The point here is that accepting responsibility is a positive thing. When outcomes are not what you intended or are negative, a sense of responsibility leads you to try and correct the situation. However, self-blame produces emotions that interfere with rational thinking and makes it hard to focus on finding solutions to a problem.

- **Values and Principles Serve as Guidelines**

A discussion of values is often left out of psychology textbooks. This is unfortunate, since values often provide us with goals that direct and guide how we think and act. Values also play a role in beliefs and motivations. They can be a determining factor when we make choices among alternative courses of action. Knowing a person's values is fundamental to understanding them, and understanding our own values is essential for knowing ourselves.

There are many types of values. We have values that involve taking care of our bodies. We learn the importance of certain actions that help increase and preserve our health and well-being. We have social values that help us deal with the people in our lives, and which lead us to behave in ways that fall within acceptable and appropriate boundaries. We learn to share, be considerate of others' feelings, treat others fairly and equitably, and respect others' property. We have moral and ethical values and principles, and very often these are bound up in our religious beliefs. The lack of attention to the role of spiritual beliefs in books on human adjustment is also unfortunate because of its centrality to human existence.

Because our values guide our behavior, they play a role in our sense of responsibility. In other words, they place restrictions on our behavior so that we make choices that are consistent with our principles. Without values, we could essentially choose any outcome we like when we weigh our options. With values, we try to operate within a more restricted system that often takes into account fairness and integrity.

We should point out that there is a distinction between *freedom* and *license*. License is doing whatever you want whenever you want to do it because you want to do it, irrespective of the consequences of your actions. Freedom means making choices based on the perceived consequences. Freedom is guided by values and principles, and implies that we accept responsibility for our actions.

• Human Beings Are Oppositional by Nature

It is not accidental that one of the first words that children learn to say in response to all kinds of requests is *NO*. It's possible that such a reaction reflects the human drive for survival and individuality. The desire for freedom, independence, and individuality is strong, particularly in Western culture. We say this in order to reinforce a point that we have made a few times already: if you want someone to treat you differently or otherwise act differently than they do, you need to invite them to consider changing by providing persuasive arguments for them to change. It is then up to them to decide whether they feel such a change is in their own interests and is something they want to pursue. You will have little success trying to force others to change how they think or act, and you're likely to end up feeling frustrated if you continually take that path. Dictators try to force change, and while they sometimes appear to be successful, keep in mind that they are overthrown at the first opportunity.

At the same time, however, no one can force us to change either. Each of us has the right to choose our own path, and just as we must recognize and honor the right of free choice for others, we must recognize that we are in possession of those same rights. Freedom of choice is something we should cherish, and we have a personal responsibility to oppose those who try to force their will upon us. Keeping this point in mind is important to feeling that we are in control of our own lives.

• Perceptions Are Not Always Accurate

We sometimes assume that what we see and hear is what really is. While this assumption is sometimes accurate, at other times it can lead to misinterpretations of events, and that can lead to problems. As we pointed out in chapter 2, perception is *tuned* by our motivations, memories, and emotions. We are not saying that there is no objective reality or that it's always elusive. We are saying that we may not always be completely in touch with it, because our perceptions can be clouded by what we expect to hear and how we feel at the moment. We need to be aware of the possibility that we might interpret things incorrectly when we interact with others. Problems that can result from misinterpretation can be avoided just by asking for clarity and checking if what you think was said is what the other person actually meant.

• Distinguish between Thoughts and Feelings

In everyday language people use the terms *feelings* and *thoughts* interchangeably. However, these words refer to different human functions. Feelings refer to emotions and thoughts refer to cognitions. This is an important distinction because it determines how effective we are when communicating with someone. If you say, *I feel angry about what you did*, we understand that this is the emotion you are experiencing. However, it doesn't describe everything that you are experiencing, nor does it explain why you feel the way you do.

Emotions can be viewed as a reaction to something. As we stated, beliefs provide the reason we feel as we do and thoughts are linked to the emotions we're experiencing. In order to clarify our communications, we need to talk about the thoughts and beliefs that accompany this emotion. Other people cannot be sure about our thoughts, in part because they may not link up the same emotions to the same thoughts as we might. If you want others to understand you, the only way to do so is by making your thoughts and beliefs heard. Communicating your emotions does not provide the basis for a discussion, but thoughts and beliefs do.

• It Is Difficult, If Not Impossible, to Change Personality

When we talk about personality, we are referring to the specific combination of inherited and learned tendencies and experiences that make us unique individuals. Personality begins to form from the moment of birth, and possibly from the moment of conception. We are all born with a certain amount of potential, that is, talents and predispositions. Our personality begins to develop when this potential interacts with our environment. Our experiences determine to what degree our potential (talents and predispositions) is fulfilled. For example, we could have the talent to become a great musician. If we are never given the opportunity to study music and play an instrument, then that potential will never be realized.

As we grow and develop, our potential is fulfilled to different degrees. This is why two people with the same talents and potential can become very different people if they are exposed to different environmental influences. Likewise, it also explains why two people who have different potentials and talents, and are exposed to the same environmental influences, can develop into very different people.

Our personality traits are firmly imbedded in each of us. By the time we become adults, it is not very likely that we can become a different person, no matter how many years of therapy or education we undergo. The permanence of these traits is the reason why people are often consistent in similar situations and why many behavior patterns, attitudes, and beliefs are very predictable. If people weren't predictable to a large extent, our interactions with them would be much more difficult. In fact, we could not have a close social relationships with others because each person could potentially behave like a completely different person each time we dealt with them. Their inconsistencies would also make it hard for us to figure out how to act with them. We gauge our styles of interacting with others by what we expect from them. We might carefully choose our words with some people because we know they tend to be highly reactive or extremely sensitive, while with others we might be firmer in our words and body language. If they're inconsistent, we would be leery about interacting with them because we might fear using the wrong or an inappropriate style.

Of course, it's also the case that people do not always behave the same way in all situations. That's because we possess a large number of traits, and some traits are dominant in certain situations while others are dominant in other situations. A person who is shy in social settings might not be shy in business or educational settings, or someone who is highly competitive in sports might be very meek when not playing sports. Consequently, while most people have consistent behavior patterns, thoughts, and beliefs that are predictable and indicative of who they are, no person is perfectly consistent or predictable all the time.

Adding to their unpredictability is their free choice and the power to change their behavior and their thinking.

Still, consistency is generally the rule with most people, and much of who we are develops early on in our lives. There is a considerable amount of research that indicates that the predisposition to respond emotionally may have an inherited basis. When newborns are in a nursery, it is clear that some are more responsive to their environment than others. It turns out that this responsiveness is predictive of adult emotionality. Babies who are very calm seem to develop into calm adults who do not respond intensely to their environment, while babies who are very responsive tend to develop into adults who respond much more intensely to people and the various events in their lives.

Psychologist Albert Ellis believed that the tendency to think irrationally is genetic, and people vary on this trait the way they do on any other trait, such as height, musical talent, and so forth. But again, heredity is only part of the picture. The expression of this trait, as with any other trait or hereditary predisposition, is dependent on environmental and learning conditions. If we have the tendency to respond emotionally with great intensity, there were probably events or conditions in our environment from the past that lead us to respond that way in the present.

While our predispositions are well entrenched, we can learn to change the way we respond to situations and events. We can change our behavior, that is, how we allow our personality traits to manifest themselves. We can also change the way we think so that we are not controlled by irrational beliefs and nonadaptive emotions. We can learn coping mechanisms and alter the ways we express our emotions. For example, if we tend to respond with anger every time we are frustrated, we can learn to monitor our anger, change our thinking about frustration, and thereby change the expression of our anger. This process will take time and a great deal of practice, but still it is possible. In fact, if it were not possible, then psychological therapy would be of no help to anyone.

It is wise to keep these ideas in mind when dealing with others, particularly in marital or other intimate relationships. Asking yourself or others to change their personality will lead to frustration and disappointment. On the other hand, asking yourself or others to change their behavior has a better chance of succeeding because we are asking them to change something that is changeable. Said another way, you have a better chance of success if you ask your spouse or others you have a relationship with to work on decreasing their inappropriate expression of anger (yelling, throwing things, name calling) than if you ask them not to get angry.

Sometimes people will use the fact that their personality traits are strongly imbedded as an excuse to justify inappropriate behaviors. A husband might say: *I am naturally excitable. When people in my family get angry or frustrated, we always yell and scream. You must understand this and let me yell and scream all I want. That's just how we handle things; it is my nature and out of my control.* This perspective is nonsense. Screaming and yelling is a behavior, a way of expressing anger, and as a behavior it can be changed. So don't let yourself or others refer to their nature or the patterns they learned from childhood as an excuse for not trying to behave in more appropriate ways.

However, although behavior can change, it is very difficult to do so. Anyone who has tried to quit smoking, switch to healthier eating styles, or tried to adopt alternative ways of expressing themselves can attest to how hard that can be to sustain. The way we behave is well-ingrained and has been our method of expression for as many years as we've been alive. It takes a great deal of repeated effort and constant attentiveness to the behavior you want to change to break such habits, and you should expect that change will come slowly and in stages.

Consequently, it is extremely important that you have patience with yourself and others. Look for small increments of improvement in the desired direction, not instant and complete change. Don't let relapses or mistakes be used as excuses for giving up or not continuing to try. You might find, for example, that you will take three steps forward and two steps backward. Sometimes we might even take more steps backward than we do forward. However, over time, and with the right amount of effort and perseverance, you will eventually find that the steps forward exceed the steps backward. Of course, as with learning anything new, the more you try, the greater the likelihood that you will make the changes you are seeking.

- **Intelligence, Knowledge, and Wisdom**

There are important distinctions between these three concepts. Intelligence is the ability to learn. We know that there are large differences among people in their ability to learn things. Many believe that intelligence may have a large inborn component, and because of that it's hard to improve this ability. The main advantages of intelligence relate to mental capacity and efficiency. The more intelligent a person is, the greater are the odds that he or she can learn something new, and learn it quickly. In a sense, intelligence can be looked at as an underlying skill for building knowledge and wisdom. Of course, high intelligence doesn't necessarily mean a person will become more knowledgeable and wiser; it just gives them a greater chance to gain knowledge and wisdom.

Knowledge refers to the accumulation of information and ideas through experience. This experience could derive from formal education, but many people accumulate knowledge over the years through their day-to-day experiences. Some people, however, don't seem to absorb quite as much knowledge as they go through their lives as other people do. A college dean once said that there is a difference between twenty years of experience and one year of experience twenty times. In other words, it is possible to grow older without necessarily becoming more knowledgeable. We might, for example, repeat the same patterns over and over again even though those patterns have not been that helpful for us. When you don't take advantage of your experiences, you don't learn from your mistakes.

The lack of knowledge is referred to as *ignorance*. We are all ignorant to some degree and we need to keep this in mind when we are interacting with others. Some people make the assumption that if they know something, everybody knows it. Others assume that if they know something, nobody else knows it. Both of these assumptions are likely to be inaccurate and can lead to problems in communication. This is especially true when it comes to dealing with your spouse and close friends. Don't assume that they know or don't know what you know. Express your thoughts clearly and make sure you understand what they are trying to tell you. Use your knowledge; that is, keep in mind that you have interpreted things incorrectly in the past and it is possible to do so in the present and the future.

Wisdom is the ability to know what to do and when to do it. There is *practical wisdom*, wisdom that helps us solve the problems of everyday life. There is also *theoretical wisdom*, wisdom about higher level issues such as morals and values. Theoretical wisdom helps us make good moral and ethical decisions. As with knowledge, age increases the probability that you will gain in wisdom, but it certainly doesn't guarantee it. While older may sometimes mean wiser, the two are not necessarily synonymous. To gain wisdom you need to pay careful attention to yourself and the others around you and try to learn from your observations and experiences.

Think about the choices you've made and the ways you interacted with others and try to identify the flaws, the ways you could have made a better choice or behaved better. Then use that information to build your wisdom. Failure to learn from your failures, as well as your successes, will doom you to repeat your mistakes and prevent you from gaining wisdom and achieving continued accomplishments.

• Understanding Our Needs, Wants, and Desires

Humans, like all other living organisms, have a variety of needs. Some of these are tied to our basic biological functions. We have certain needs that are governed by our biological mechanisms, and they serve to ensure our survival. We all need food, liquid, and other substances for our bodies to function properly. The food we consume is converted into blood sugar that is used by the cells in our bodies to carry on the functions to maintain our bodies. There is a center in the brain that monitors blood sugar and when it falls below a certain level we experience the sensation of hunger. In lower animals, the experience of hunger is always followed by food-seeking behavior and then eating when food is found.

That's not always the case with people. Although the sensation of hunger works the same in humans as it does in other organisms, eating behavior is also governed by psychological and social factors in humans. Eating not only satisfies our biological need for food, it also satisfies a number of other needs, and these needs can determine when and what we eat. For example, we have social customs that govern our eating behavior, and we use feeding as the basis for some social interactions, such as dining out with friends or enjoying the holidays with our families. Humans go on diets, eat to celebrate, and may starve themselves to death for a cause. In other words, we have a lot of rituals that surround food and these extend well beyond its fundamental biological purpose.

Many of the behaviors that go beyond basic biological functioning are governed by our beliefs and thoughts. For example, we go on diets because we believe that losing weight will give us valued results, such as better health, increased attractiveness, and improved self-esteem. All of the basic biological needs in humans work much the same way. Meaning, there is a biological basis for the need, but the behaviors that we actually engage in to satisfy that need can be governed by psychological and social factors.

Not all needs have the same degree of importance to us. In fact, it has been postulated that needs are in a hierarchy. We must satisfy biological and safety needs before we can seek to satisfy more psychologically based needs. This makes sense in that extreme biological deprivation will interfere with thinking processes. It's very hard to think about taking part in most kinds of activities if we are hungry or thirsty. We first must eliminate the hunger or thirst before we can then concentrate on other things.

In addition to those that are biologically linked, humans have a large number of other needs that seem to have nothing to do with basic survival. It is not clear whether these needs have a biological cause like hunger and thirst, but they seem to have been present in all cultures throughout time. As just a few examples, we need to be with other humans, we want to have something to do in our lives that we believe is important, we want to love and care for someone and have an intimate relationship, we want to be valued by other people. It would be useful for you to spend time thinking about your own needs and make a list for yourself.

Sometimes the word *needs* is used to refer specifically to biologically determined processes, while the words *wants* and *desires* are used to refer to more psychologically based processes. We prefer not to make this distinction because we would argue that *all* human needs, wants, and desires have a strong psychological basis.

The psychological processes that are beneath our wants, needs, and desires are our beliefs. We believe we'll receive certain benefits from having our wants, needs, and desires satisfied, and it is in anticipation of receiving these benefits that we continually strive to have them fulfilled. If you want to understand what someone wants, needs, or desires, you must understand her thoughts and beliefs. Within the same vein, if you want to understand your own wants, needs, and desires, you must look for the beliefs that lie beneath them.

Understanding these underlying beliefs is important because it lets you understand whether or not wants, needs, and desires can be fulfilled. Much of what we seek is supported by rational beliefs. However, some goals may be based on irrational beliefs, even if we don't think they are. As the major distinction, rational beliefs can be satisfied and irrational ones cannot. When irrational beliefs aren't satisfied, we can experience maladaptive emotions, such as anger or frustration. By identifying them as irrational, we can then discard them and avoid the pain of having them unfulfilled.

Humans also have a strong need for *meaning*. Whenever something happens, we all want to have an explanation for why and how it happened. Very often we don't have much difficulty understanding why or how something has occurred. However, some things that happen are not easily understandable, and when they're not, we sometimes will resort to inventing an explanation. We might appeal to some outside force when something bad happens for which the reasons are not readily apparent. For example, some people believe that many things in life that happen to them are determined by unseen or supernatural events outside of themselves (God, Nature, Angels, Spirits, etc.). Such beliefs provide an explanation that satisfies their need for meaning. Others believe that every human act creates an energy that will produce an outcome that has consequences. They believe that if you do something good or bad, then something good or bad will happen to you in the future. The idea here is that some outside force will pay you back for what you have done. One version of this idea is the concept of *karma*. There are other versions of this idea, all of which provide meaning for those who are faced with events they don't understand.

We may sometimes want to surrender to the impulse to look for paranormal reasons for events we're surprised by. However, we're better off resisting that urge. Such explanations may cause us to believe that many aspects of the world are more beyond our control than they actually are. As we have pointed out many times, when we believe we have no control, we can deny our own responsibility for some things, and we may feel helpless to improve other things in our lives.

- **Everyone Make Mistakes**

One of the fundamental principles about human beings is that they are fallible and they make mistakes. Failure to accept and work with this principle can be a source of unhappiness, depression, and misery. If we are continually upset with ourselves for making mistakes, we have set our expectations too high. We will often be disappointed in ourselves and therefore hold negative thoughts and beliefs about ourselves. Furthermore, not accepting the fact that human beings make mistakes can lead people to deny their mistakes or blame them on others. When they do that they deny another fundamental principle of being human, that we are responsible for our actions.

When we truly accept the idea that mistakes will happen, we have a much easier time forgiving ourselves, and that means we're less prone to suffer guilt. As we have pointed out, guilt is a nonadaptive emotion that makes it difficult for us to focus on fixing problems that come from our mistakes.

Acknowledging our own fallibility is certainly important, but it's just as important to do the same for other people. If we don't allow for the possibility that others will make mistakes, we can be disappointed and find it hard to accept their apologies and willingness to make amends. As a result, we may find it difficult to maintain positive feelings about them and that will interfere with our ability to enjoy our relationships.

- **Avoid Dwelling on Past Failures**

We all spend some of our time thinking about the past. While some of these thoughts might be pleasant or nostalgic, more often than not we tend to focus on negative past events. We all have made mistakes in the past and have had bad things happen to us. It's not abnormal, and in fact can be healthy, to review these situations in our minds and learn from them. That's how we build our base of knowledge and wisdom.

However, it's not healthy to spend so much time thinking about the past that we leave little time for living and acting in the present. Spending too much time going over past mistakes can lead to ruminating, that is, reviewing past negative events to the point of obsession. Ruminating can especially become a problem when we experience traumatic events (e.g., child abuse, destructive parenting, etc.). As we mentioned in a previous chapter, negative thoughts and nonadaptive emotions can lead to a cycle of negativity. That's precisely what happens with ruminating; it fuels itself, so that negative thoughts start a chain reaction of negativity that's hard to break. The negative emotions that it produces can waste valuable time that could be used doing productive and positive things.

Ruminating stems from irrational beliefs. It is not a logical or rational process because past mistakes or negative events cannot be changed, nor can we alleviate the unpleasantness surrounding them. Albert Einstein was quoted as saying that the operational definition of insanity is doing the same thing over and over again and expecting a different result. The best we can do with past mistakes is to learn from them and put them away, and then try to avoid making the same ones in the present and the future.

For some of us, this is easier to say than to do. One must vigorously fight the temptation to dwell on past negatives. Nevertheless, persistence will generally win out, so keep working at it and you will make progress. For those who continue to find that the past intrudes on day-to-day living, we recommend seeking professional help. This is particularly advisable if the past events you're stuck on were particularly traumatic, or you find an urge to repeat a past action that resulted in failure as an attempt to get it right the second time (this urge for repetition is called *repetition compulsion* by psychoanalysts).

• Forgiveness Heals

As we interact with people it is likely that some of those people will do things to us that we consider harmful. It is not uncommon to become insulted, hurt, angry, or have other similar reactions to this perceived harm. We use the term *perceived* here because we want to emphasize the personal nature of how we interpret situations. Not everyone will interpret the same action as harmful. An offhand comment from another person might be ignored by some but taken as a major insult by others. When we lean toward the latter interpretation, it is not uncommon to hold a grudge against the person whom we perceive as having harmed us.

Ethical codes and most religious doctrines tell us that we should be forgiving to those who harm us. This advice certainly has its socially redeeming qualities, but it's also sound from a psychological perspective. When we hold a grudge and refuse to forgive, we leave ourselves open to the danger of ruminating about the event, and that's especially likely to happen if the harm came from someone we regard as important to us. As we rehash the episode in our minds, we experience all the negative emotions, and perhaps some behavioral outbursts. Yet the hurt remains because the event cannot be repealed. Holding grudges is a lot of wasted work and destructive to our well-being as well as our relationships. Most important, when we hold a grudge we give power to those we believe harmed us and feel less in control of our lives because we're focusing inwardly on the hurt and not outwardly on our own lives.

As we've mentioned, ruminating has its roots in irrational beliefs. We might be thinking, *How could this person have done this to me? What's wrong with him or her? What's wrong with me?* This easily translates to, *This person should not have done this,* and, *If they did this, they must be bad, or I must be bad.* Grudges sometimes will also lead to revenge, which is a bad idea that has no utility. It has been suggested that taking revenge is like drinking a cup of poison and expecting the other person to die.

In trying to forgive a wrongdoing, there are a few steps that you might consider. First, acknowledge your pain and talk to others about it. Don't deny or apologize for your thoughts and emotions. Then try to appeal to your rational side and don't let irrational beliefs or nonadaptive emotions get in your way. Keep in mind that forgiving is something you are doing for yourself. You will feel better and more in control of your life when you drop the anger and are no longer being ruled by nonadaptive emotions.

Again, like most change, this can require some real effort and lots of repetition. Nevertheless, the advantages to your psychological health far outweigh the costs. Forgiving someone for a perceived harmful act does not mean that we need to continue our relationship with that person. It does mean that we will try to have this event exert less and less effect on our present and future thought processes.

• Learn to Tolerate Frustration

People vary in the degree to which they can tolerate frustration. Some people can have a large number of things go wrong in their life and are still able to adjust to them without experiencing a great deal of stress and negative emotions. Other people are readily frustrated by anything large or small that goes wrong. They experience a great deal of stress and negative emotions to these events. Dr. Ellis referred to those people who have very little tolerance to frustration as having *low frustration tolerance* (LFT). LFT is a particularly difficult problem because it is hard for a person with LFT to confront negative emotions. Instead, they usually do whatever they can to get away from frustration by employing denial or leaving the situation.

Learning to improve your tolerance for frustration is essentially learning how to cope with failure. When things are not going according to our desires, reacting with anger or withdrawal won't make the source of our frustration go away. Instead, we are better off trying to be proactive by finding ways to deal with the event and its circumstances. If you are experiencing negative emotions, such as anger or frustration, because you have not achieved your goals, focus on your beliefs. You might discover that you believed improvement would come more quickly or easily. If that is your irrational belief, you can adjust your thinking about how fast or easy changes can be achieved. Focusing on the right reasons for your frustration can lead you to experience more appropriate reactions in the face of adversity.

As we have stressed a number of times, we are all capable of rational and irrational thinking. Effective thinking requires that we monitor and pay attention to our thought processes. When we do so, we will get to know ourselves better and at the same time give ourselves the opportunity to find ways of ridding ourselves of some irrational beliefs and thinking patterns. The better we know ourselves, the more we can make free choices that meet our true needs, and the more effective we can be in coping with life's various obstructions.

• The Tyranny of *Shoulds* and *Musts*

The essence of irrationality is trying to describe human behavior in absolute terms, which is precisely what is implied when we use the words *should* or *must*. These words also imply demands. Human beings can be oppositional, have the ability to think and choose, and can never be absolutely controlled. In other words, most people don't think they *should* or *must* do anything. We would be better off if we removed the concepts *should* and *must* and the ideas they represent when we think about ourselves and other people.

Of course, as with all things human, there are exceptions. These words are adaptive when they are meant to persuade rather than demand. This would be the case when *should* is used to mean something that would be good for us to do. However, we always have to keep in mind that our intention is to persuade. If we use the word *should* to imply an absolute demand, then we create unrealistic expectations. Simply recognizing what is best for us or others does not guarantee that our or others' behavior will follow suit, nor should we expect it to. Human beings *should* take care of their health, but they can choose not to. Every smoker knows that he or she would be much better off not smoking, but they still smoke. If human beings *should* or *must* never make mistakes, they wouldn't, but they do.

Instead, it is much more helpful to think in terms of the possibility that human beings will do what they choose to do, regardless of our suggestions. When we make provisions for the possibility of outcomes other than what we desire, we manage our expectations so that they're more in line with reality. In that way we're not disappointed, nor are we upset that we can't get people to do what we want them to.

We would like to make a distinction between *shoulds* and *musts* and what theologians and philosophers call the *moral ought*. Moralists and ethicists realize that human beings need descriptions of moral behavior framed in absolute terms. You can't have a commandment that says, *If you think it's a good idea, don't lie.*

With that said, even the *moral ought* is really a guideline for human behavior, not an absolute command. Commandments and such are written without expectations as to what people will actually do. In fact, if people always did what was moral, right, and best for the greater whole, we wouldn't need commandments, rules, laws, or principles.

A reasonable distinction between our personal usages of *should* and *must* and the *moral ought* has to do with ownership. For the latter, we may try to live within the guidelines of commandments, but they are not ideas that we have created. In contrast, when we use *must or should* regarding our own or others' actions, the demands they imply come directly from us, that is, we own them. We then use them to set expectations about behavior, and we set standards that might not be attainable. When these expectations aren't met, we can feel frustrated, angry, and disappointed. Such nonadaptive emotions don't help you solve problems; they get in the way of solving problems.

We would also like to make a distinction between absolute necessities and conditional necessities. Absolute necessities state that situations *must* or *should* be the way we want or believe they should be. Stating our expectation in this manner is irrational because there is no reason why the world or other people *must* do what we want it or them to do. Conditional or logical necessities are produced by setting up conditions. For example, if we want to graduate college, we must pass all of our courses, but we don't *have to* graduate college.

By decreasing our *shoulds* and *musts*, we have more control over our own lives. We have a better chance of understanding and exploring our choices and then freely making those choices. If we give up our freedom and insist that we and other people *must* behave a certain way, we will live under the tyranny of *shoulds*. We establish a set of expectations about our own and others' behavior that can lead to nonadaptive emotions, and these can be harmful to our psychological well-being and the quality of our relationships with other people.

SUMMARY

In this and the three previous chapters we have covered a number of important issues about the link between thinking patterns, emotions, and behaviors. We discussed how certain patterns can improve and others can detract from your personal happiness and your relationships with other people. This model is consistent with many philosophical and scientific understandings of human nature and will help you to understand yourself and others from that perspective. We suggest that you review these chapters often to get a good understanding of this model and work at building some of what was discussed into your own ways of thinking.

5

THE BASICS OF TAKING CONTROL

Most of us would like to change something about ourselves. We would like to lose weight, stop smoking, have a more satisfying relationship with our spouses, overcome our anxiety and depression, and so forth. We see these issues as obstacles to our happiness and enjoyment of life, and we think things would be better if we could just figure out how to make the changes.

Unfortunately, many of us have a hard time changing things in our lives. We might think that we have no power over certain things that we do or things that happen to us. Others may think events and situations are a matter of fate, believing that the good and bad things in their lives are predestined. When people think they cannot affect their lives, they believe that they are helpless, and that sense of a lack of control can work against their emotional well-being and can block them from doing something about the things that are the source of their unhappiness.

As we have stressed a number of times, life is a process and things are constantly changing and not always in the manner we would predict. We get older every day; our bodies change. We learn some new things and forget some old things. We choose to engage in some activities and pass on engaging in other activities. We never wake up as completely the same person that we were yesterday.

We have also stressed that we can change some things but other things we cannot. Many of the events that occur in the world around us have some random qualities to them and occur on the basis of probabilities. There are also events in the world that have causes that are unknown to us and also events that have causes that are known to us but over which we have no control. However, circumstances and situations are not predestined.

Some people might prefer to believe in predestination or fate because it makes dealing with the issues in their lives easier. Predestination or fate means that some force (God, the Universe, Nature, etc.) determines what happens to us. When faced with an unpleasant situation, we can cope better if we believe that situation happened because it was predestined to happen. If this is true, then we are personally in the clear because we could not have done anything to prevent the situation, and therefore we are not responsible for the outcome. Sometimes believing in predestination or fate is a way of reconciling ourselves to the fact that bad things occur through the fault of no one, especially us. Thinking this way gives us a way to understand why things happen and lets us avoid taking responsibility for things we can control.

Unfortunately, none of it is true, and believing in predestination or fate is not so far away from believing in magic. Here's an example to illustrate how events that are suggestive of predestination are in fact explainable through the laws of physics. Suppose a bee stings a person driving a truck, causing him to lose control of the vehicle. The situation occurs in a flash, and a pedestrian on the sidewalk with no time to react gets hit by the truck. Some may believe that it is fate that the pedestrian was hit by the truck. However, we would argue that bees, trucks, and pedestrians are everywhere, and while the random combination of the three meeting up at a given point in time might be extremely rare, it's certainly not outside the realm of the possible. It might be a case of unfortunate timing for the pedestrian, the truck driver, and the bee, but it is not fate. Believing in predestination or fate is not a good idea, because it limits your sense that you have control over your life.

In the above, the situation is out of the pedestrian's control. Sometimes we can control outcomes. Now suppose a different person is walking through a neighborhood. That person looks down a street and sees a truck at the opposite end of the block driving erratically. He or she might even see the truck driver waving his arms frantically, as if he was swatting at something inside the truck. If that person chooses to walk down that street and gets hit by that truck, that's not fate and it's not random, it is cause and effect. The thought pattern that produced the decision to walk down the street increased the likelihood of getting hit by the truck. So while there's not much that could have been done about the truck hitting the first pedestrian, choosing not to walk down the street could have led to a different outcome for the second one. Our point with the above examples is that some things can be changed and others we have to accept, but fate has nothing to do with it.

The things that we can control with any degree of certainty really come down to our personal thoughts, behaviors, and emotions. These are the things that we own, and just as we cannot control the thoughts, feelings, and actions of other people, with few exceptions no one can tell us how we should think, act, or feel. We can't just pay lip service to this fact; we must *truly believe* that we have freedom to make our own choices, within the bounds we've talked about earlier, and that we are in control of our thoughts, actions, and emotions. This is a rational belief and one we must first own before we can gain control over those aspects of our lives that can be controlled.

CHANGE

Once you've absorbed the point that you do have the freedom to choose, there are a number of ideas and methods for you to use to help you gain more control over some aspects of your behavior and emotions. However, before getting into these techniques, you need to understand something about change. Often we are unsure as to how to make the desired changes happen. Sometimes we know how to change things but find it too difficult to do the things we need to in order to make changes. Using an example we brought up previously, there is no mystery as to how to quit smoking. You just stop putting cigarettes into your mouth and lighting them up. We're also well aware of the dangers of smoking to health, so we have the motivation of a longer life to help get us to quit. Sounds easy, but anyone who has tried to stop smoking knows how difficult it is to do. The desire to smoke, along with all of the external influences (e.g., friends smoking, its stimulating benefits, etc.), sabotage our efforts. The result is that we find ourselves continuing to smoke.

For some people, the problem is that they expect that having insight into a problem will easily allow them to make changes. Unfortunately, knowing what needs to be done will not magically compel us to do it.

We are ignoring the fact that many human behaviors are very complex and understanding how to change them is not so easy. We may also fail to realize how difficult it is to change habits. Habits are well-ingrained patterns of behaviors that have been woven into the fabrics of our everyday lives.

Others may focus on the wrong aspect of a problem when searching for a solution. For example, many people would like to lose weight. We need to eat to live, but how do we control our eating so that we can lose the weight we want to lose? Losing weight involves changing our eating and activity habits, and only by changing our habits can we achieve sustained weight loss. Going on a diet that lets us shed a few temporary pounds but can't be sustained over a long period of time is not a real solution to our weight problem. That's because we haven't changed how we think about food and eating.

Change must begin with a focus on our thought patterns, and that can only happen through self-monitoring and self-reflection. Introspection and retrospection are the tools we have at our disposal for understanding how we think and what we believe. Some people might believe that if they want to change, they should focus on an emotion or a behavior and work on changing that. However, as we have pointed out in chapter 3, it's important to remember that emotions and behaviors are caused by beliefs. Therefore, it is best if we focus on our belief systems, which are at the core of how we act and feel, as the pathway for changing our behaviors or emotions.

We should note that it is possible that changing behavior and emotions can lead to changes in beliefs. However, from our perspective we prefer to work with beliefs as the primary agents of change. If we keep in mind that behaviors and emotions spring from beliefs, then unless we change the beliefs we have not eliminated the cause of the behavior or emotion. Consequently, the old behaviors or emotions can return because they are the ones that are consistent with the beliefs that we're still holding on to.

Let's consider again trying to lose weight. Suppose that when we were growing up we learned to associate food with family closeness, or certain foods such as candy were used as rewards for good deeds or actions. From our upbringing, we have developed a belief about food that goes beyond its life-sustaining purpose; it includes emotional benefits. If we don't try to change our beliefs about food and its link to emotional benefits, we will eventually return to the same pattern of eating. That's why diets that focus just on the behavior, such as reducing calories or avoiding certain foods, are not effective for many people over the long term.

PROGRESS

There is also the issue of how to gauge improvement. When people try to change, they usually keep track of their progress by observing the occurrence of the behavior or emotion they are trying to change. For instance, people who want to overcome depression will note the occurrence or lack of depressive episodes that they experience within a given time period. If they begin to count fewer incidences of depression, they will judge themselves as having made progress in overcoming their depression. As soon as their depressive episodes return, and they inevitably will, these people will then judge themselves as having relapsed. Patients often complain to their therapist that they were feeling much less depressed, then something happened, and now they are *back to square one*. Their conclusion is that they have made no progress at all.

This way of looking at progress when it comes to learning new patterns is an example of *all or none,* or *dichotomous thinking.* It is a very unrealistic view of how change actually takes place, and it can be at the root of thinking and behaviors that work against achieving your goal. For one, it can lead people to think that they have failed, and that may lead them to give up trying to change. An inaccurate perspective on progress can also lead to a sense of powerlessness. Patients who think they have relapsed will often begin thinking that things cannot be changed or that they don't have what it takes to make changes, and so they are destined to live with their problems forever.

The experience of failure can also add problems beyond just a sense of powerlessness. For someone who is depressed, failure can cause them to be more depressed than they were before. This is referred to as a *secondary disturbance*, that is, disturbing oneself about being disturbed. It is common for people who are experiencing negative emotions to upset themselves about their experience. People can get themselves depressed about being depressed, anxious about being anxious, depressed about being anxious, and so on. Secondary disturbances are in reality another layer added to problems that then have to be dealt with. In order to make changes in such situations, it becomes necessary to deal with the secondary disturbance first before the primary disturbance can be dealt with. That compounds the problem and lengthens the time before real change can be realized.

Rather than think about personal improvement as a continuous upward event, it's much better, and much more realistic, to think of it as an up and down process. We get better, drop back a little, get better, drop back, and so forth. Real progress is not a steady upward linear effect; it's more accurately described as a sawtooth curve. The graph in figure 5.1 shows two curves that demonstrate realistic and unrealistic expectations about change:

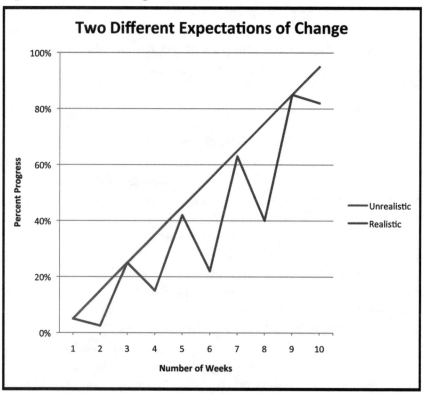

Figure 5.1.   Realistic and Unrealistic Expectations of Change

The straight line represents an unrealistic expectation of change because it shows a steady increase over time with no steps backward. The sawtooth or jagged curve, on the other hand, represents a more realistic expectation. This curve shows that improvement is typically followed by some sliding back, which is then followed by improvement, and so on. When we have the expectation that change is a sawtooth curve, we come to realize there will be gradual improvement over time. However, at any one moment, one might be doing a little better or a little worse. We might even find that as we try to change something, we actually get a little worse in the early stages. As an important point, that perspective reduces some of the pressure on us. If we allow ourselves to believe that change can be slow and that sliding back is extremely likely, if not inevitable, we're less likely to get frustrated and give up trying.

Another point that is useful to keep in mind: problem behaviors and emotions are not one-dimensional. It is not just about how often such behaviors or emotions occur. In fact, we can think of behaviors and emotions as having three dimensions; frequency, duration, and intensity. Within a given time period, we experience a behavior or emotion a certain number of times (frequency). These behaviors or emotions last for a defined period of time (duration) and they vary in how strong they are (intensity).

When we assess whether or not we're making progress, we should think in terms of these three dimensions. For example, if we are trying to reduce our depression we first must observe how often within a given period of time (let's say a week) we get depressed, how long each episode of depression lasts (duration), and how deeply depressed we get (intensity). A realistic expectation of progress would be that over time we get depressed less frequently, for shorter periods of time, and/ or less deeply.

However, be aware that we don't have to change all three dimensions at once to make progress. Again, you should expect success to come in increments, not all at once and not in every way. Change on any one of these dimensions should be taken as a good sign that things are moving in the right direction.

When it comes to zeroing in on something you want to change, people often find it difficult to remember the three dimensions of frequency, duration, and intensity of their behaviors or emotions. To avoid this problem, it is best to keep a written record of what you want to work on. Each day make specific notes about your beliefs, behaviors, and emotions. Try to record how long the belief, behaviors, and emotions last (duration) and how strong (intensity) they are. While keeping records might seem a bit tedious, it's the best way to monitor your progress. Besides, when you see the results of your efforts on paper, even if they're only minor improvements, you might be surprised to find just how motivated you will be to keep working.

As we've mentioned numerous times throughout, trying to change old habits and patterns takes a lot of hard work and perseverance, and to expect that change will be instantaneous or easy is tantamount to believing in magic. Magic is best described as action without work. We watch a magician place a blanket over a person, he or she then says a few words and that person disappears. The magician has not expended any effort that we can detect to make the person disappear, it just happened. Wouldn't it be nice if we could change things about our-selves just by wishing them to be different?

THE BELIEF IN MAGIC

Most of us can't help but wish magic were real. As proof, all you need to do is to go into any bookstore and go to the self-help section. Count the number of books on losing weight, quitting smoking, having a better sex life, or changing any other difficult-to-deal-with pattern of behavior. Look at all the books whose titles suggest that change is easy. How many times have we seen a title such as, *Eat All You Want to Eat and Still Lose All the Weight You Want to Lose*? As silly as this sounds, books like these often become best sellers. If you want to make money, write a book on how to magically change some difficult-to-change habit. No matter how absurd your method, people will buy it, because they want to believe it's that easy.

Unfortunately, magic doesn't happen. The truth is changing habits takes planning, thinking, and a lot of effort, and most important, perse-verance. We need to come up with a plan and stick with it through all of the ups and downs. We also need patience. Even though we may ac-knowledge that it won't happen overnight, we may still be unrealistic as to how long it can actually take to change some behaviors. Habits have staying power, and they have that because they have provided us with benefits over the years. If you need to lose weight, you probably love food or profit emotionally from eating; if you smoke, you probably do it because it feels good. Because habits are rewarding in themselves, and change can be slow and difficult to achieve, it's so much easier to give up trying when success isn't coming as we would like it.

COPING

That brings us to the issue of coping with failure. Life events can be classified into three groups; positive, negative, and neutral. A positive event involves a pleasant situation (getting something you want). Positive events are usually accompanied by intense positive emotions (joy, pleasure, elation). Negative events involve unpleasant situations (conflict, deprivation, loss) and are accompanied by intense negative emotions (anger, depression, anxiety). Neutral events involve neutral situations (walking uneventfully down the street) and are usually accompanied by only mild or moderate emotional reactions.

Within the framework of trying to change something in ourselves, failing to achieve our goal can be looked at as a negative event. When that happens (as it will because humans make mistakes), we can experience corresponding negative emotions, such as anger, frustration, or impatience. To reiterate our point in chapter 3, the emotions we experience stem from our beliefs. The type of belief (rational or irrational) will determine whether the emotions are adaptive or nonadaptive. With respect to change, an irrational belief might be that we should have achieved or gotten closer to our goal than we have at a given point in time.

Coping comes into play when we are faced with a negative life event. People have various ways they can cope with such events, and some approaches are more effective than others. From one perspective, coping can be either active or passive. In active coping you do something to deal with the event and/or its circumstances. In passive coping you withdraw, that is, you try to avoid dealing with the event and do nothing. We always cope with a negative situation by either actively dealing with it or withdrawing from it. Active coping is the more effective way to approach negative situations, because you are confronting the situation head on and that gives you an opportunity to come up with a solution. Passive coping, on the other hand, is rarely of any value.

Coping can also be either emotion focused or situation focused. When coping is emotion focused, our efforts are exclusively aimed at trying to reduce the negative emotions. When coping is situation focused, our goal is to try to reduce or change the irrational beliefs and thoughts that cause the negative emotions. Of the two, situation-focused coping is more effective. Drinking, taking drugs, gambling, and other similar activities are emotion-focused coping behaviors which only temporarily reduce negative emotions but eventually create their own problems.

As we have mentioned earlier, changing something in ourselves requires that we focus on the thought patterns and beliefs that are at the root of the thing we want to change. Situation-focused coping helps us identify the irrational beliefs and destructive behaviors that cause the nonadaptive negative emotions. We can then work on replacing these with rational beliefs. In so doing, we can reduce our nonadaptive negative emotions.

Keep in mind that coping is effective when it reduces the negative emotions by dealing with the beliefs that caused them. It is ineffective when it does not reduce negative emotions, or when it increases the negative emotions by reinforcing the irrational beliefs. You might, for example, still experience nonadaptive emotions such as anger or frustration, even after you thought you had identified the underlying irrational belief. If that's the case, then it is likely that you have not truly uncovered the belief that is driving your emotions.

When it comes to effective coping, very often we experience negative emotions because we are not further along in reaching our goal. The irrational belief is that improvement should have come more quickly or easily. If that is your irrational belief, you might want to adjust your thinking about how fast or easy changes can be achieved. The right coping skills can help you set up more realistic expectations about your goals and make it easier for you to persevere in the face of adversity.

SUMMARY

In this chapter we discussed the issues you need to consider as you try to get more control over your life. It is important to understand the concepts of change and progress and to keep track of our thinking and behavior so that we can realistically evaluate our efforts. It is also important for us to avoid the human tendency to believe in magic and to look for or expect easy and quick solutions to complex problems. Finally, we need to understand that all reactions to life situations are attempts to cope with these situations. Learning how to use effective coping skills when faced with a negative event can help you stick to your plan in order to reach your goal.

6

CHANGING YOUR THINKING PATTERNS

At this point you should have grasped the idea that learning to take control over your life is likely to require that you learn how to change your thinking. We have touched upon how our thinking patterns and beliefs determine how we interpret situations and events, as well as how they can affect the types of emotions we experience. In this chapter, we delve into the specific ways you can get more in touch with your thought processes. Achieving that goal is an important step in learning how to change your thinking. From there you can identify and dispute your irrational beliefs and replace them with more rational ones.

SELF-REFLECTION

As one of the key points from the previous chapter, learning about your thinking process requires self-reflection. Self-reflection means listening to that voice inside of our heads that speaks during most of the time we are alive. We give ourselves a lot of material to work with because we're always thinking. We experience thinking as an internal monologue. Even when we sleep, we experience the internal monologue as dreams.

Self-reflecting means carefully listening to that monologue and analyzing the content in terms of what it means to you. It would be worthwhile to listen not only for the words but also to the tone and intensity of your internal monologue. You might try speaking your thoughts out loud in a private place so that you can hear the full impact of what you are thinking. You might even try recording yourself as you speak aloud and play it back to yourself at some later time. You will be amazed at the amount you can learn about yourself from this simple exercise.

Self-reflecting also means reviewing previous events in your mind, things that have happened to you and situations you found yourself in. Think about the decisions you had to face and the choices you made, and the beliefs that popped into your mind and guided those decisions. Think about the emotions you experienced when you were in various situations. Then try to uncover what thoughts and beliefs triggered those feelings.

IDENTIFYING EMOTIONS

Each of us experience a variety of positive and negative events, and we have certain emotions that are associated with each of these types of events. Emotions are very complex experiences that are an important part of life. In fact, life would be pretty boring without emotions. They add flavor to day-to-day living the way spices add flavor to food. When events are positive, our emotions are also positive, and we feel on top of the world and in control of our lives.

However, when something negative happens to us, that's when we're likely to run into problems. We will experience an intense and negative internal dialogue that reflects our thoughts and beliefs about the negative event. We will simultaneously experience strong negative emotions like anger, fear, or disgust. Our negative reactions to these events can also affect us physically. When people get angry they often experience pains in their stomach, headaches, and other physical reactions. They may also become agitated, move around a lot, strike out at something (punch a wall), and perform other outward physical acts.

Along with physical reactions, there will be a large amount of negative thinking. This negative thinking causes us to get angry and can cause us to ruminate about the event, repeating it over and over again in our minds, and get locked into a cycle of negativity. As such, negative emotions are not just tied to the immediate event that we're reacting to; they can be retained in our minds for quite a while, sometimes causing us to feel bad for days.

Because our beliefs cause our emotions, we have to identify and evaluate our beliefs in order to change our emotions. However, in order to uncover our beliefs, we have to work backward. We first have to examine the emotions that emerge before we can identify the beliefs that caused them. In other words, we have to think about how we feel so that we can then figure out what caused us to feel that way.

Albert Ellis distinguished between two types of emotions, *appropriate* and *inappropriate.* As stated previously, we prefer to call the two types *adaptive* and *nonadaptive* emotions. Adaptive emotions are those feelings that enrich our lives by highlighting and magnifying our experiences. They include feelings such as joy, sadness, and happiness. Nonadaptive emotions, on the other hand, detract from our functioning. They include things like depression, anger, anxiety, and jealousy. Nonadaptive emotions get in the way of our day-to-day living. They interfere with every aspect of life because they interfere with our thought processes. If not dealt with adequately, they can create chronic problems and lack of productivity.

While this distinction might be readily grasped, it's not always easy to identify emotions correctly. In fact, people often experience a nonadaptive emotion and label it as adaptive. This is especially true with an emotion like anger. Since anger is often viewed as undesirable or inappropriate, we will often say that we are annoyed when really we are angry. The difference between the two emotions is not just intensity but a difference in kind. Annoyance is experienced as an unpleasant negative emotion that passes in a short period of time. However, annoyance is considered to be an adaptive emotion and that means it typically has a rational belief behind it.

As an example of a rationally based annoyance, a person might say to her friend: *I really don't like it when my husband comes home late without calling. I think that he is not being considerate of me and I better talk to him about it and ask that he consider changing his behavior.* The rational belief expressed here is that people will sometimes not consider others when it would be better for their relationship if they did. There is no insistence that others *must* change their behavior. There is only the expression of the desire that it would be helpful if they did change their behavior.

On the other hand, anger is much more intense and doesn't derive from rational beliefs. Instead, anger will have irrational beliefs as its main underpinning. It will often lead to repeated negative thoughts that will dominate one's thinking and feelings. For example, the wife might say to her friend: *My husband is an inconsiderate, thoughtless person who never thinks of anyone but himself. He should realize how much this upsets me and he must change his behavior.*

There are a couple of irrational beliefs working in this example. For one, the wife describes her husband in absolute terms (he never thinks of anyone else) and demands that he behave differently (he must change). As she mulls over the situation, she is likely to find herself ruminating, that is, reviewing the other occasions in the past when her husband has been inconsiderate, which further feeds her anger. Her mode of thinking will most likely lead to an outburst when the husband finally arrives at home, and this outburst will most likely lead to fighting and other negative behaviors.

We should point out that very often arguments that stem from irrational beliefs rarely find their way to solutions. Partners will generally resort to an attack-counterattack approach, which often causes an argument to escalate. It's not unusual for couples to develop a pattern that over the years follows this same path, because each partner comes to expect that their conflicts will include accusations and other forms of negativity that can extend far beyond what the original argument was about. When such communication styles become habits, the damage can be far-reaching, affecting all other aspects of the relationship.

IDENTIFYING IRRATIONAL BELIEFS

We can identify our irrational beliefs by asking ourselves three basic questions. The first question is: *Is this belief logical?* A belief is not logical if it cannot be supported by evidence or falls outside what is accepted as the bounds of human experience. For example, any belief that contains a *should* or a *must* cannot be logical because these concepts are absolutes and do not describe human behavior.

The second question is: *Is this belief consistent with my experiences?* Suppose we believe that other people should do what we want them to. Since there are likely to be many occasions when they have not, that belief clearly does not fit with our experiences. The third question is: *Does holding this belief help me obtain the goals I have for myself?* A nonadaptive emotion prevents us from solving a problem. So holding any belief that causes us to experience nonadaptive emotions does not allow us to attain our personal goals. If, in examining a particular belief, your response is no to one or more of these three questions, you have to conclude that the belief is irrational.

Suppose we believe that we must have the love and approval of all of those whom we regard as important in our lives. This belief is illogical on a number of grounds. For one, we cannot give reasons why this *must* be. Since we are probably having this thought after having been rejected by someone, it clearly does not fit with our experiences. Also, holding on to this belief will upset us and may cause us to act in a way that will not make others feel very loving toward us. So this belief does not help us attain our personal goal of being loved.

Be careful! Sometimes irrational beliefs are more subtle than the one that we discussed above. Suppose someone demands approval not from everyone but just one particular person or group of people. That is no less irrational than demanding that everyone love and approve of you No one *has* to do anything, including loving me, no matter how much I *demand or want* it. In a similar vein, suppose we don't demand that we never make any mistakes but demand that we just not make a particular mistake. Again, the world, people, or events in it are not going to cooperate just because we *demand* it—even of ourselves.

Here's another example of how difficult it can be to identify irrational beliefs. A very close friend recently experienced circulatory issues and required that two stents be inserted into an artery. Before this procedure, she was an extremely outgoing individual with an easy smile and a great sense of humor and was generally in an upbeat mood. Afterward, she would at times appear sullen and seemed to experience brief bouts of depression. In trying to uncover the source of her emotional issues, she suggested that maybe the stents signaled to her that she is getting old and is mortal. But in further discussions, it seemed she was more concerned that a major health problem would mean she might not be able to help her children, all of whom are in their midthirties and doing quite well on their own.

Coming to terms with one's mortality is understandable and tends to strike some people hard when they enter their sixties. While this is something she needs to overcome, we wouldn't classify a fear of dying as irrational. However, the fear that she won't be able to help her children suggests an underlying irrational belief that her children cannot get by without her help, which is clearly not the case. While that seemed liked the answer, further discussions suggested that it wasn't so much that she worried that her children needed her help. It was more the case that she needed to feel as though she was a help to her children. The irrational belief here could be a fear of rejection by her children, because if she is not helping, she might not have any value to them.

We are not saying that you can't have preferences, even very strong preferences, as to how you would like things to go. We are saying that demanding or expecting such things will get you into trouble. When we prefer something, we are prepared for the possibility that we might not get it and can make appropriate plans for choosing alternatives. When we demand something, we are not prepared for not getting what we want. In fact, we expect things to go the way we want and we don't make alternative plans. This lack of preparedness can only lead to extreme frustration, anger, and other destructive and inappropriate emotions. Demands and commands rarely work unless you have a large army under your control. However, even then there are no guarantees.

LEARNING TO DISPUTE IRRATIONAL BELIEFS

Once irrational beliefs are identified they need to be disputed. This involves having a long and frank talk with yourself. Your goal in this conversation with you is first to admit that the belief is irrational, and second, to provide yourself with countering rational beliefs. Self-talk in many cases may need to be *strong* and *forceful* because irrational beliefs are well ingrained and have a tenacious quality. You need to point out to yourself how this belief is illogical and destructive to you in many ways. Such strong talk helps you accept situations as they really are even when they are not the way you want them to be. It also gives you room to plan alternatives and make provisions to deal with these situations in the most constructive way that you can.

There are, of course, a large number of possible irrational beliefs, probably as many as there are people on the planet. Nevertheless, we thought it might be useful to provide a few examples of the more common irrational beliefs along with their rational counter beliefs. You might find it useful to study table 6.1 in order to help you identify your own irrational beliefs and also to help you find effective countering rational beliefs. You might also consider using this list as a catalyst for coming up with your own list of irrational beliefs and rational substitutes.

To become truly proficient at countering irrational beliefs, it takes careful personal examination and a lot of practice. In fact, it will probably be necessary to have the same talk with yourself over and over again for each belief you're trying to change. Don't put yourself down if that's your experience. Human beings are fallible, mistake-making organisms, and irrational beliefs are deep-seated in our psyches.

Instead, give yourself permission to accept who you are so you can concentrate on decreasing your irrationality. Once we are able to identify our own *musts* and *shoulds,* we can change some of them to preferences and desires. This allows us to reduce our frustration and the inappropriate emotions that sap our energy and inhibit our ability to work toward rational and obtainable goals. The more we are able to make our expectations more rational and realistic, the less unhappy we will be and the more productive and satisfying our lives will be.

Albert Ellis coined a few words so that his patients would remember the important concepts they represented. These words helped to get a patient's attention and emphasized the irrational thinking that the patient was exhibiting. For example, he referred to a person's tendency to repeatedly insist on things being what they want them to be instead of what they are as *musterbating* and *shoulding.*

Here is a good example as to what Dr. Ellis meant. Suppose a patient reports to his therapist that his brother failed to show up for his birthday party and that as a result he was really angry at him. He tells the therapist that his brother's failure to attend his birthday party is disrespectful and selfish. Suppose, also, that the patient repeats over and over again in therapy that his brother must be respectful and considerate of him. He also tells the therapist that this thought about his brother was constantly on his mind.

When a patient would repeatedly insist that something *must* or *should* happen in a certain way, Dr. Ellis would tell the patient that he was *musterbating* or *shoulding* on himself. These particular plays on words are not only easy to remember, they also help to emphasize the negative and self-destructive aspects of irrational thinking.

Table 6.1.   Examples of Irrational Beliefs and Countering Rational Beliefs

Irrational Belief	Countering Rational Belief
I can't stand it. I hate when things go wrong.	I may not like what is happening, but I can stand it. I have stood for it in the past and I will in the future. It may not be pleasant, but I can get through it.
Why do people make unreasonable demands on me?	People are often self-centered and make demands that meet their own needs. They are not necessarily trying to get one over on me. I can choose to comply with some or none of their requests. If I choose to comply, it is not their responsibility.
Why don't things in my life go smoothly?	The world is a crazy and unpredictable place that I can't control. I would prefer if things went smoothly, but I can handle the problems. I have in the past; I will in the future.
Why don't people do things my way (or the right way)?	People do whatever they want to do. I can't control others. It would be easier for me if people did what I wanted them to do. They don't have to and I would be better off not demanding that they do.
Why is life so difficult and why are so many things going wrong?	Life is a process that has its ups and downs. I may be in a down time now. If I keep focused on how bad things are, it will take longer for things to improve. If I try to emphasize what positive there is, the down time will pass faster and I will feel better.
I don't want to do what I'm doing now.	I can choose not to do what I am doing if I want to pay the price for not doing it. I can't do anything without consequences. This includes doing nothing. If I choose an action, I choose the consequence. I choose my own pain.
Why did I make that mistake? I should know better. I can't make mistakes like that.	People are fallible. I cannot prevent myself from making mistakes. I can fix what I can when I make a mistake. I can accept what I can't fix. The more time I spend worrying about a mistake or possible mistake, the worse it gets. It's like picking at a sore. It never heals.
Why can't I make myself understood? Why doesn't anyone understand me?	Not everyone can understand everything I or anybody says. Maybe people understand me, but they don't agree with me. Maybe I am being unreasonable and I need to listen to others.

Dr. Ellis also coined the term *awfulizing* to refer to a person's tendency to think of every negative event as the worst thing that ever happened to them or anyone else. Again, the purpose of this coined word is to help the patient recognize her own irrational thinking and become aware of the negative impact it has on her. When we *musterbate and awfulize*, or we *should on ourselves*, we spend all of our time focusing on the negative events and do not spend the time to decide what we can or cannot do about these negative events.

Dr. Ellis referred to those who have low frustration tolerance as suffering from *Ican'tstandititis*. As mentioned above, this is a particularly difficult problem because those with it often avoid dealing with negative events, nonadaptive emotions, and the irrational ideas that cause them.

INTERNAL MONOLOGUE VERSUS INTERNAL DIALOGUE

As we mentioned earlier, most of us experience our thinking as an internal monologue. Sometimes we might think the thoughts we have are beyond our control. People often say, *I can't help what I think. The thoughts just happen.* Or they might say, *I know some of my thoughts aren't rational, but that's what I believe and how I feel.* When such rationales are used, we actually deny we are responsible for our own thoughts and that we can choose to think differently if we want to. However, actively engaging in a frank dialogue with yourself about such beliefs gives you the opportunity to take back responsibility and control of your feelings.

An important point to remember is that we all strive to be happy and nonadaptive emotions will always get in the way of that goal. Consequently, when experiencing a strong nonadaptive emotion you might ask yourself: *Do I want to continue to feel this way?* If you don't, and you shouldn't, you need to change the way you think or else these emotions won't pass. Remember, you need to be honest and very forceful with yourself, and at the same time be patient. These thoughts will return over and over again and you need to fight them repeatedly.

As an aid to learning, try speaking out loud, and better yet, record your dialogues and listen to them as many times as you can. When you start thinking things that lead to negative emotions, or you hear them from your recording, dispute them as vigorously as you can. You can use some of the rational disputes that we have listed in the table in this chapter, but you can also make up your own. Whatever works, do.

SUMMARY

This chapter addresses the key issue of self-reflection and learning to analyze one's thinking. Our objective is to help you identify those irrational beliefs that can be the source of some of our problems. We presented some of the more common irrational beliefs held by many of us, and offered examples of more rational beliefs that can serve as effective substitutes. We also addressed the general approach to disputing these irrational beliefs that can help you reduce the impact and occurrence of negative emotions.

7

INTERPERSONAL RELATIONSHIPS

Right from the beginning, human beings have tended to congregate in groups. In fact, Aristotle was one of the first to argue that human beings are social creatures by nature. We live together in groups and depend on others for many of the things we want in life. We use our social circle to define ourselves and feel connected to the world at large. Our close relationships provide emotional support for us and can add to our overall enjoyment and well-being.

Relationships with others are so important that it's in our best interests to develop the right skills to get the most out of them. In the next three chapters, we will cover some of these skills, and we will point out ways the tools and strategies we have been discussing can be applied to your dealings with others. Understanding the issues in social relationships will make them more rewarding and fulfilling. We suspect you will also find that improved social effectiveness is another means by which to gain control over your life.

THE RELATIONSHIP CONTRACT

In every relationship with other people, we have an unwritten contract. By a contract we mean we have a set of rules, expectations, and boundaries that define that relationship. The standards that operate in these contracts can vary, depending upon the type of relationship we have. The contract we have with a spouse would be very different from one we have with a friend, and that contract would be different from the one we have with a casual acquaintance. The contractual aspects of each relationship have implications for how we interact and communicate with that person.

Contracts also serve the purpose of defining the roles we hold. Roles are like jobs, in that they specify certain rights and responsibilities. We all have many roles. We are sons or daughters, bosses or employees, fathers or mothers, friends, cousins, club members, and so on. It might be useful to take some time to think about all of the roles we have in our lives. In doing so, we will probably be amazed as to how many *jobs* we really have.

Whenever we take on a new role, it is wise for us to consider first the rights and responsibilities that come with it. That's what we would do if we were interviewing for a paying job. We would ask about the job responsibilities and about our rights, that is, the benefits and compensation. In this way, we can make an informed judgment about whether we want to make the commitment involved in taking the job. If we make incorrect assumptions about either our rights or responsibilities, we risk making a contract that we will not or cannot live up to. Said another way, if we take a job and we made the correct assessment of our rights and responsibilities, we will mostly like the job and find it satisfying. If we've made the wrong assessment, however, we'll soon be back in the job market. Such a lack of clarity before making the decision might be considered a bit foolish.

The same approach should be used before deciding to enter any contract, even including intimate relationships. It is of fundamental importance that we spend as much time as possible examining what our expectations are for ourselves and others with whom we have relationships. We need to spend time alone and time together discussing as many aspects of our relationship as is possible. If we do this, we will have a better idea of what it is we are agreeing to when we make our contract. If not, problems will undoubtedly arise. We will be fortunate if they are solvable problems.

PRINCIPLED SELF-INTEREST AND THE PERSONAL AGENDA

In order to understand how contracts work in personal relationships, we need to address the concept of personal agendas. Most of us are brought up with the idea that there are two ways to approach the world. We can either be selfish or selfless. *Selfish* means that you put your wants and desires first, no matter what the consequences are to other people. You never allow anyone to impose upon you and what you want is the sole motivation for your behavior. Needless to say, a person who acts selfishly will end up having very few friends, if any. People will avoid such a person because there is very little that can be gained from a relationship with them. *Selfless* means that we never acknowledge our own wants and desires no matter what the cost to ourselves. We put everybody's needs before ours, no matter how unimportant they are or who they are.

A person who tries to be selfless may also not be in high demand. That's because we can have a hard time trusting them. Appearances to the contrary, we might believe that selfless people really want something; they are just unwilling to say so or are hiding what they're really after. It might be especially difficult for most of us to like someone whose selflessness appears to be noble and good, when we really think that they are not being noble and good. In effect, many people who appear to be selfless are really being selfish. They have just disguised their agenda. Sometimes they don't disguise their agenda very well.

The hard truth is that we all have an agenda, because we all operate with our own best interests in mind. We all need and want things and these things are usually in accord with the values and beliefs that we hold. Some of what we want may include material goods and services, and others may have to do with our broader social and ethical values. That is, we may want to see peace in the world, others prosper, and people behave ethically and responsibly toward each other. Some may have to do with how we are perceived; that we are loved or respected by others.

To have an agenda is a good thing; it is normal and sensible. Again, however, we always need to keep in mind the difference between what we want and what we demand. Remember, demands are unrealistic and irrational and rarely get fulfilled, and they can be especially trouble-some when we try to apply them to our relationships.

It is a good idea to spend some time thinking about what it is that we really want in life. You might try writing out a list of things that are on your agenda. As you do, keep certain principles in mind. Some of these things we're likely to want now and some are more long-range goals. Goals have different values and importance to us and it is a good idea to take that into consideration when making your list.

As we think about the things we want and need, we may tend to focus just on individualistic goals, such as success at our job or losing weight. However, having good relationships with others should have a very high value and priority as both immediate and long-range goals. If these are not at the top of your list, you deny the very essence of what it means to be human, that is, to be connected with other people. If our relationships are not given the highest priority in our lives, we're not as likely to give them the time and attention they deserve. Without the right amount of effort, it may be difficult to make them as fulfilling as we would like them to be.

THE UNCONSCIOUS ASPECTS OF OUR AGENDA

Discovering our agenda may not be as easy as it might seem. We may not be able to list all of the things we really want or need because some things may not be in our consciousness. Sometimes we're not conscious of things we want because we have never thought about it. For exam-ple, most of us want the love and approval of others, particularly those whom we love and of whom we approve. While this may not make our list, it is a reality for most people.

There are various reasons why things we want and need aren't easily recognized. Some of our desires might escape our consciousness be-cause they are threatening to us. It can be easier to push these ideas and goals out of our awareness than to deal with wanting them. This is often true about sexual matters. Many people are threatened by their own sexual desires and would prefer to deny and avoid them rather than admit they exist and deal with them. However, letting such important life issues go unexamined and unexplored can lead to problems. You won't be able to make free and thoughtful choices that satisfy your needs, and you may not feel your relationships are as fulfilling as you would like, although you might not be able to figure out why you feel that way.

We also may not want to recognize certain goals and desires because we believe we do not have a right to ask for or want them. This can stem from a lack of self-confidence or from a long history of being told that certain goals are beyond what we're entitled to. For example, for many centuries, social pressures have forced women to deny their own sexual needs, or they were told that they did not have the right to an education or a career. It's important to recognize that we have a right to our own needs and desires so that we can deal with them in appropriate ways.

There may be other desires that we are conscious of but are afraid to admit them to ourselves because we think we will be rejected or ridiculed. You may want to be successful in your career but will downplay that desire because you have a low opinion of yourself or you believe that stating a wish to be successful makes you appear conceited or overly ambitious.

Despite these potential barriers, it is important for our personal well-being that we try to understand our own agenda as completely as possible. As one of the primary benefits of knowing our personal agenda, it lets us come up with the specific rights and responsibilities we want in our contracts. Being aware of such details is important for all relationships, but especially those that are more intimate, such as a marriage.

Unless we are fully aware of our own needs and desires, we cannot work at having them fulfilled. The result is we really cannot enter into a meaningful and beneficial contract with anyone else, because we don't know the terms of the contract. Getting there may take a great deal of self-reflection and discussion with others in our lives. Keep in mind that a full recognition generally happens slowly, so having expectations to the contrary will be counterproductive.

THE INTERPERSONAL CONTRACT

It is fairly easy to see the details of our contracts with business or casual relationships. These are usually pretty straightforward, with not a lot of nuances. However, we may find it harder to think about the contractual terms for our intimate relationships. It's essential that you try to do so, preferably before you enter into one, but if not, late is better than never. You may find, for example, that you have agreed to do things that you really don't want to do. Or you might discover that you have some needs that your partner may not be aware of, and others that you have identified through self-examination but your partner is either unwilling or unable to fulfill.

Unconscious Aspects of the Interpersonal Contract

Just as we all have unconscious aspects of our agenda, we can have unconscious aspects of our interpersonal contracts. There are things that are clearly part of a relationship contract but may not be conscious to either party. These things often involve negative behavior patterns in which each person is motivated by inappropriate negative emotions.

Here is an example of what we mean by unconscious negative patterns that might be inadvertently built into a contract. There was a woman who was married to an alcoholic. She complained that he would pick a fight with her over some trivial issue and he would nag her until she got angry and yelled at him. At that point he would storm out of the house and go get drunk. He would then return to the house when she was sleeping. He would make a great deal of noise, with the purpose of waking her. She would get up, yell at him, and tell him to go sleep in the guest room. The next day she would wake up and feel guilty for throwing him out of their bedroom. She would then try to be nice to him and things would calm down. She said that this arrangement had been going on for years.

It was suggested to her that this pattern of behavior reflected part of her marital contract. Her husband used her anger as a justification for his drinking. He also used her guilt as a way to avoid having to confront his problem. She got to express her anger at his drinking and paid for her anger with her guilt. Many patterns like this have a clear unconscious contract, and that is what maintains them. If there was no contract, that is, if both partners had not been unknowingly accepting of this pattern, it wouldn't persist.

Because they tend to be associated with negative behaviors and emotions, the unconscious aspects to every relationship contract are often at the center of problems. Only by identifying the unconscious, or less obvious, terms of these contracts can people discover the destructive patterns that may be lurking in their relationship. They can then try to change their expectations of the relationship and adopt more positive ways of dealing with the negative emotions and behavior they produce. Without examination, unconscious contract terms that are not dealt with will persist and will, at best, diminish a relationship, and at worst, cause it to end.

When we understand all aspects of our own agenda, we can make sure our contract is not loaded down with negative patterns and that our personal needs are satisfied. This understanding also allows each partner to make known their needs. Armed with such knowledge, couples have a better chance of meeting each other's needs.

Knowing each other's full agenda also lets both partners know the needs their relationship may not provide for. The truth is very few marriages are capable of satisfying all the needs of both partners. As we've mentioned, sometimes we may not want to do some of the things that our partners want us to. Or each partner's needs may run counter to each other. For example, one partner might like to spend a lot of time with friends while another prefers to stay at home. Knowing such differences in each other's needs puts you in a position to come up with solutions that serve the interests of both.

NEGOTIATION IN RELATIONSHIPS

When needs and agendas are out of sync, it follows that couples would do well to learn to negotiate some of the terms of their contract. They may also need to keep an open mind so that these terms can be renegotiated when necessary. The concept of negotiation may seem odd to you when applied to an intimate relationship, but it actually fits quite well. In fact, there is a good deal of evidence that shows couples in happy marriages do a lot of negotiating with each other. The failure to recognize the key role negotiation plays can cause problems if one or both partners feel their relationship is not meeting their needs.

A marriage counselor had a patient who taught negotiation skills for union people. When confronted with the idea of negotiating with his spouse the patient seemed rather put off. He said that he thought it was a good idea to negotiate in business relationships but not in a marriage.

The counselor then asked him some questions about what the patient taught regarding negotiation skills. Specifically, the counselor asked the man if he taught people to (1) be clear about their agenda, (2) treat each other with respect and equality, (3) be honest and straightforward, (4) be willing to give and take, and (5) be willing to consider the possibility of changing when presented with a reasonable contrary point of view. The man replied that of course he did. The counselor asked the man why he thought this would be an inappropriate way to deal with his wife. The man clearly recognized the counselor's point.

This example illustrates not only the reasonableness of using negotiations in relationships, but also describes how it should be done. Notice that the first step is the identification of your own agenda. As we pointed out, this is difficult to do and is a process that requires constant monitoring and careful attention to our thoughts to discover what it is that we really want. Only from that point is it possible for you and your partner to begin the negotiating process.

Before discussing negotiation in more detail, we would like to point out the difference between negotiation and compromise. Suppose two people were planning a two-week vacation together and one person wanted to go Florida and the other wanted to go to Alaska. After much discussion, one person suggests that they should compromise. They get a map of the United States and a ruler. They then measure the distance between Florida and Alaska and pick a point as close to the middle as they can and decide to go there on their vacation. Given the types of environments that Alaska and Florida offer, it's not likely that either partner will be happy with the choice of somewhere in the Midwest.

In compromise, neither person believes that they have gotten what they want and therefore neither is satisfied with the solution. On the other hand, in a negotiation each person gets something they really want in exchange for giving in to something their partner really wants. A negotiated solution for the traveling couple might be that they spend one week in Florida and one week in Alaska. Each person can believe that he or she has given something to the other person without being deprived or cheated.

Negotiated solutions work much better than compromises on a lot of levels. For one, both come away with feeling their needs are satisfied. They also get an opportunity to feel like they are giving something to the relationship and that makes them feel more committed to their partner. And because each partner also feels better about the other, they tend to treat each other better, and they feel better about the future of their relationship or marriage.

Of course, other negotiated solutions could have been equally effective in the above scenario. It all depends on each person's agenda. For example, a husband might agree to go to his wife's destination of choice in exchange for being able to do things he enjoys, such as playing golf or fishing. It doesn't matter what the actual solution is as long as the principle is followed that each person gets something that they want and also gives up something for the sake of the other person. As a useful exercise, you and your partner might try to come up with situations in which you initially disagree and then try to come up with different possible negotiated solutions that can work for both of you.

Negotiations are particularly useful when it comes to conflicts, the inevitable by-product of two people living under the same roof. Conflicts in marriage can be looked at as problems that need to be solved together by both people in the relationship. If these problems are not successfully resolved, they can remain a source of division and irritation between the couple. If these irritations accumulate, they can be destructive to the relationship because they're like sores that never heal. Couples who leave problems to fester may find over time that they grow apart and may come to believe their marriage is not worth the effort.

Through learning how to negotiate, it's possible to eliminate many of the issues that can damage a relationship over the long term. To this end, we present a series of steps that might help you through the negotiation process. Although we've listed them in a specified order, this should not be regarded as fixed. Think of negotiation as a process and be flexible in implementing steps as you need to. However you approach it initially, with practice you and your partner will find the way that works best for you.

STEPS IN NEGOTIATION

Step 1: Discover Your Own Agenda

No one can negotiate effectively if they don't have a clear idea what they want in life and what their priorities are. Knowing your own agenda gives you a context for dealing with and resolving problems and issues. That's because very often the problems that arise in marriage are a result of unmet needs. Use introspection and self-talk to discover your agenda; you will get to know yourself better and come away with a much better idea of what you want. You will have a clear idea of what you are negotiating for, and you won't be sidetracked by incidental issues. The more you get to know yourself, the better you will be at negotiating.

Of course, for negotiation to be truly effective, your partner must also know their own agenda. Otherwise, they won't know what they should be negotiating for, and that means they could end up agreeing to things that in fact they don't want or might not get things that they really feel they need.

Step 2: Define the Issue to Be Negotiated

When we are confronted with a problem in a relationship, we must make every effort to state the problem in a clear and precise way. As a general rule, try to frame problems in terms of what people do (behavior) and not who they are (personality). You can only negotiate about what people might do, not about their personality characteristics. You can negotiate about how money is spent, but you cannot negotiate about a person being too frugal or too careless about money any more than you can negotiate your height or age. As we've mentioned, personality is difficult, if not impossible, to change, but behavior can be changed. Besides, stating a problem in terms of personality can be taken by your partner as an attack on his or her character in general. When that happens, he or she might feel the need to retaliate by taking shots at your character and that causes the argument to escalate and move off the original point.

People in a relationship will sometimes use an individual conflict as an opportunity to express their frustration and dissatisfaction with their relationship in general. It is as if all the issues of their relationship that are unpleasant and/or unresolved are carried around in a big bag. When a specific issue comes up, they dump the entire contents of the bag onto the floor and each other. Many of these issues will probably have nothing to do with the problem at hand. Consequently, the negotiation process has to be suspended because you are no longer talking about a single issue.

In these situations people can sometimes resort to name calling and attribute their inability to solve a problem to the personality shortcomings of the other person. For instance, suppose a couple has two dinner invitations for a Saturday night. In trying to decide which one to accept, the discussion becomes heated and one person says to the other, *You always insist on having things your way. You are stubborn, just like your mother.*

There is no appropriate response to this statement. If you tend to be stubborn and that is a consistent pattern of behavior for you, not much can be done at that particular moment to change your stubbornness. Later on you could work on being more open to alternative ways of thinking. Also, whether or not you learned this behavior from your mother is irrelevant, and that kind of comment only fuels anger.

Instead, what is needed is a specific account of the problem. For the above situation, the couple should focus specifically on the situation at hand. They might state that they have two invitations for Saturday night dinner which conflict. They both can acknowledge that each dinner engagement might be more attractive to one person than to the other. They should also respect the fact that each has a different and a viable opinion about the issue. Respect is important, because without it you won't communicate on an equal footing or take your partner's point of view seriously.

Step 3: List the Points of Agreement and the Points of Disagreement

Once you have agreed upon the specific issue to be negotiated, stay on that issue only and then decide what aspects of the issue you agree on and which ones you do not. For the example given above, you might agree that you would both like to go out for dinner on Saturday. You might also agree that either place would be acceptable, if you had had only one invitation. You then could agree that each of you has a different first choice.

Step 4: List the Alternative Courses of Action

The next step is listing the possible alternative ways that you can proceed. You need to be creative here. They could include not doing anything, since no decision is a decision to keep things as they are. Even unlikely or absurd alternatives are worth exploring since they often give perspective to a problem. You could consider flying to Paris for Saturday dinner, or suggest calling the governor or the president of the United States and ask them to make the decision. Of course, these are not serious considerations, but absurd or unlikely alternatives inject humor into the situation and that can lighten the moment and reduce the chances of the discussion escalating into a full-scale battle.

We should note that when attempting to be humorous, make sure your spouse knows that's what you're trying to do. You know your spouse well and should have a good idea what is humorous to them. Still, sometimes humor can come across as hostile and offensive if it's insulting or cutting. As long as what you say is interpreted as humor and not personally offensive to the other person, it is a good way to break any tension, and reduced tension can help the negotiation process.

It is wise to spend a good deal of time listing the alternatives. Sometimes the best solutions don't occur to us immediately, and there are usually many more alternatives than are initially apparent. If they were all obvious, you probably wouldn't need to negotiate. For example, you might decide to call one of the parties and see if you could get a rain check. You could invite both parties to your house for dinner, or you could go out to dinner with everyone. You need to work together to discover them. Working together is the essential ingredient that transforms a conflict from an argument into mutual problem solving.

Step 5: List and Prioritize the Positives and Negatives for Each Course of Action

Once you have listed as many alternative courses of action as you can, the next step is to list the positive and negative outcomes for each possibility. These outcomes will very likely be different for each person so it is wise for both to make a separate list. Keep in mind that each alternative can also vary in importance, and what's important can be different for each person. For example, having a friend annoyed at you for turning down a dinner invitation may be less unpleasant than having an aunt scold you for turning down a dinner invitation. On the other hand, being scolded by your aunt for turning down a dinner invitation may be much more unpleasant for you than it is for your spouse.

Specifying the negative and positive outcomes of each alternative allows each person to understand why the other thinks the way that they do about the conflict. With better understanding, each person in the relationship can make a more informed choice. They can take into account the other person's thoughts, emotions, and values in their decision.

People sometimes don't recognize that there are positive and negative outcomes to choosing NOT to decide. On the positive side, you don't give anything up or accept something you don't want. On the negative side, you risk building up resentment in yourself and the other person because you don't really resolve the conflict and that can cause tension and unpleasant feelings to linger.

Step 6: Decide Which Alternative Is Most Acceptable to Both

After all the alternative courses of action are laid out, evaluated, and discussed, it will be easier for both partners to reach a negotiated solution to their problem. Again, the overriding principle in a negotiated solution is one in which each spouse feels he or she is getting something they want and at the same time giving something to the other.

Unfortunately, not all problems have positive or happy solutions. Sometimes the best solutions are not necessarily those which are most pleasurable. For the example above, the best solution for the couple mentioned above might be to turn down both dinner invitations. This may not be a pleasant choice for either person, but it might be the best choice if the other choices have many more unwanted negative outcomes. If both partners have agreed to the decision, they at least have solved the problem and reduced the chance the conflict would escalate. The important point is that the couple made the decision together, with full consideration of each other's thoughts, beliefs, emotions, and values.

Keep in mind that if this process is to be effective, solving the problem together means that each partner has to feel like they own the decision. That is, they cannot feel as though the decision was forced upon them or that it was arrived at unfairly. If both partners don't feel they had equal input, one or the other might resent the decision. Resentments tend to be held onto and may come out at other times and in other aspects of the relationship.

Step 7: Make a Plan to Implement the Negotiated Solution

Once you have chosen an alternative course of action, the next step is to devise a concrete plan for implementing that course of action. At this point we need to focus on being realistic. Solutions that cannot be implemented because they're not practical, or have other reasons why they won't work, are not very useful.

Suppose it is decided that taking everyone out to dinner together is the best solution when choosing between two competing dinner invitations. There are a number of issues that need to be dealt with that would follow from this choice. What type of food will be most acceptable to everyone? What restaurant should we choose? How much will the dinner cost? Can we afford it? Is the restaurant conveniently located for all of us? What will be our contingency plans if one of the parties does not want to go?

There are probably a few other issues that have to be considered other than those we listed. It would be a useful exercise for you to try to come up with others, because with practice you'll get better at it. Note that completeness at this stage is essential, so take the time you need to come up with as many issues as you can. If you happen to miss some important issues, you could very well make the wrong decision and put both of you back to square one.

While these seven steps provide a broad outline for reaching a negotiated solution, there are a few additional points to keep in mind that will help you negotiate effectively. For one, emotional arousal can be a hindrance. It is best not to try to negotiate when you are upset (e.g., anxious or angry). When emotions run high, we don't think as clearly as we should and we tend to be more reactive, so it is best to wait until everyone involved has calmed down before you begin the process.

On the other hand, don't use your emotional state as an excuse for avoiding issues. If you continually say that you are too upset to discuss or negotiate an issue, you may be trying to avoid confrontation. Time will tell if this is the case because the person avoiding the confrontation will never be willing to negotiate.

Secondly, some things are not negotiable and not all problems are solvable. Most people have certain basic principles they will not violate under any conditions. For example, many of us believe that cheating on someone with whom you are in a committed relationship is not an acceptable behavior. All the talking and negotiating in the world will probably not lead to an acceptable solution if one partner sees this as something they want to pursue and the other doesn't.

This example is of course extreme, but it points out how important it is that people communicate and negotiate about as many issues as possible before they get into a committed relationship. In this way they can determine if there are underlying problems for which there are no solutions and which will always be present in the relationship. Having seen many separations and divorces, we can say with certainty that a bad premarital breakup is much better than the best separation or divorce. Consequently, it is best for those who can't negotiate solutions to meet their needs to end their relationship.

Finally, a truly negotiated solution will make an issue go away. Sometimes people in a relationship will reach what they think is a negotiated solution, only to find that the same issue surfaces later on. This usually indicates that someone was not able or willing to stick with the negotiation process until an acceptable mutual solution was found. Within this vein, forcing a solution never really works. You cannot solve problems by intimidating your partner into agreeing with you. On the other hand, giving up and giving in never really works either. People who think they can solve their problems by making decisions that don't satisfy both partners are just delaying an explosion. Remember, you can't feed an alligator to keep it from eating you. You will run out of food, stamina, and patience. And the more you feed the alligator, the larger it gets, and the bigger its appetite gets. What will you do then?

SUMMARY

In this chapter we have emphasized the importance of viewing each of our relationships as contracts, having rights and responsibilities. To come up with the terms of each contract, you need to know your agenda, the things that you want and need from your relationship. You also need to understand the agenda of the other person, especially if the relationship is an intimate one, such as marriage. Only by understanding each other's agenda will you have an opportunity to meet the other person's needs and desires and to have your own satisfied. Remember that many of the difficulties couples face in their marriage are a result of unmet needs.

When we run into problems in our relationships, we believe they can best be resolved by coming to a negotiated solution, that is, a solution in which each person gets something they want and willingly gives something to the other person. We have laid out a step-by-step procedure that we think will help you in the negotiation process. You and the other person with whom you are involved will undoubtedly modify this procedure to fit your relationship. Finding a way that works best for you is fine, as long as you stick to the general principles of negotiation that we described above.

8

EFFECTIVE COMMUNICATION

In the simplest of terms, communication refers to the transmission and reception of information between and among people. For sure, human beings are not the only species that communicate. There exists an extensive literature on communication across the broad spectrum of non-human species, including insects, monkeys, whales, among many more. Understanding and analyzing communication is critical for the understanding of human relationships. We can think of communication as the *food* for relationships. Relationships in which communication does not exist, or in which the communication process is *spoiled*, will eventually wither and die.

While our definition certainly gets at the core of things, it belies the fact that communicating with others is a highly complicated process. There are volumes written on the nuances of how people transfer information between each other, and it's impossible to do justice to the topic in this brief chapter. Instead, we focused primarily on the principles of *effective communication* and how they impact the quality of our relationships.

MODES OF COMMUNICATION

Communication involves many aspects or modes of information transmission. Most of us think of spoken language when we think about communication. This is far too limiting an idea and it does not provide a complete picture of what it means to communicate. For example, communication involves both verbal and nonverbal aspects. All of us are familiar with how much information we can pick up and send out through facial expressions, body posture, and hand gestures. In fact, nonverbal communication is just as important and just as rich in content as what we convey with words.

However, we caution you about relying too heavily on the information that you obtain from nonverbal sources. A facial grimace could represent anger, displeasure, or stomach gas. The truth is we need to be careful in interpreting all of the messages that we pick up from each mode of communication, verbal and nonverbal. As previously stated, there is a particularly special relationship between emotions and perception, and perception plays a role when we process information. For instance, negative emotions such as anger and anxiety *narrow* perception and prevent us from taking in all of the information available in our environment. This narrowing effect makes it difficult to process information effectively and very often will lead to miscommunication. That is why you're better off not trying to solve problems or engage in any difficult task when you are highly emotionally aroused.

COMMUNICATION INVOLVES INFORMATION PROCESSING

Because perception can impact on interpretation, it is not correct to assume that the message that is intended is the message that is sent, nor that the message that is sent is the message that is received. When we communicate to another person we may not be aware of the depth of our messages. If we are angry at another person and are answering a factual question, we might not only provide an answer to that question but will also communicate our anger by our tone of voice, choice of vocabulary, body posture, or gestures.

As the potential for miscommunication is always present, it is wise to consider the possibility that the message we think we got might not be what was sent or, more important, what was intended. As a general guide, it is important that we confirm our interpretations of what people are saying before we draw firm conclusions or act on them. The simplest way to confirm a message is to ask the person with whom we are communicating if the message that we received is what they thought they sent. Failure to do this, particularly in intimate relationships, can lead to unnecessary conflicts, hurt feelings, or other negative consequences for both parties.

Communications can include many different types of information. We can convey facts, as well as thoughts, emotions, and beliefs. When we communicate our thoughts, we are using our internal cognitive processes to present statements about realities as we understand them. If I say, *that chair is red* or *I don't have any money*, I am trying to communicate something that I perceive to be a reality. This reality may not be objective or true, but it is what I am experiencing.

Transmitting our thoughts to others is an important part of communication, but it is not the *whole ball game.* Communication has to be two-sided and involves receiving information from others. When we hear and understand the thoughts a person presents to us, we are learning about them. When there is a give and take of ideas and thoughts, we are exchanging information and we are communicating. Only through communicating, that is, the two-way exchange of information, are we able to reach some understanding or agreement with others during conflicts. When the information exchange is one-sided, we're not really communicating.

When we take in information from others, we're not just recording it; we're processing it. As we discussed in our chapter on perception, human beings continually take in and process information from their environment through all of their senses. The processing part is where we change and transform many aspects of the information we receive to conform to our own experiences, motivations, expectations, and memories. We often see what we expect to see and what we are used to seeing. This is what we refer to as *tuning* of perception.

Tuning has some very positive effects but can also have some real negative effects. This is particularly true if what happens is not what we expect or want but is nonetheless something important for us to hear. It's not uncommon to hear people say that they have repeated certain things over and over again to another person and that other person *just didn't get it.* Sometimes it's really a matter of the other person just *not wanting to get it* because the message would be too burdensome or unpleasant. *Perceptual tuning* can cause us to misinterpret or miss completely important cues around us.

The truth is with so much going on in the information transmission and reception process, there's a lot of room for things to go wrong. Without realizing it, we can send messages we didn't intend to and pick up messages that weren't intended. When our communications skills aren't as precise as they could be, we can inadvertently harm our relationship. In fact, many of the difficulties that couples run into in their marriages have more to do with how thoughts and ideas are presented and less to do with the specific issues themselves. Ineffective communication can cause problems that we could have avoided, and some of these problems can be another basis for feeling we lack control over our lives.

Nevertheless, it is possible to improve our communications skills, thereby maintaining control in our relationships and allowing them to develop and prosper. To this end, we have outlined what many consider to be the primary elements of effective communication that can be useful in any interpersonal situation.

• Communication Must Be Interactive

Although communication can, in certain circumstances, be primarily unidirectional, as in a lecture or speech, effective communication in relationships needs to be bidirectional. In fact, we would argue that effective communication is always bidirectional. Even in a lecture, only the most insensitive speaker is unaffected by the verbal and nonverbal behavior of his or her audience.

Communication requires action from all participants. In all interpersonal relationships, the give and take from each participant is the only way we know that the person we're speaking to cares about the issue at hand and what we have to say about it. However, some people have a particularly difficult time dealing with situations that are negative or confrontational. Instead of actively engaging in discussion, they withdraw, either by saying nothing or working desperately to change the subject. When they do this, they miss the opportunity to present how they are *feeling* and what they are thinking, as well as the chance to be an advocate for their rights. This leaves a problem unresolved and opens up the possibility of misinterpretation by the person with whom they are interacting.

When we avoid or refuse to give input to a conversation, particularly if it is confrontational, we can also send a negative message, even though that might not be the intention. Withdrawal can be easily interpreted as indifference, insensitivity, anger, or other equally destructive ideas. That can lead the other person to distance themselves emotionally or give up trying to fix a problem, which leaves them feeling as though their needs are not being addressed.

- **Don't Let Emotions Get in the Way**

While our tendency might be to attack a problem as soon as it arises, sometimes it's wise to wait, especially if the issue is particularly important or provokes strong negative emotions such as anger, fear, or anxiety from either participant. In a previous chapter we spoke about how emotions can affect the way we perceive things. Emotional arousal narrows our perception, so we have a greater likelihood of misinterpreting messages. Trying to communicate when you are experiencing intense negative emotions will often create situations that are undesirable. We might say things in the *heat of the argument* that we don't mean but that are nonetheless hurtful and damaging.

If we take a *time-out* when we are experiencing these intense negative emotions, we will communicate much more effectively. Waiting allows anger and other negative feelings time to decrease in intensity. When we calm down we will think more clearly and can approach a conversation in a more rational manner. So if emotions tend to run high, give yourselves some time to *clear your heads* before you engage in a difficult discussion.

However, we should also keep in mind that a time-out isn't forever; we still have an obligation to deal with the issue at hand. Sometimes we might decide to not speak to the person with whom we're in conflict, but that's done not to calm down but to make them feel rejected. That's not a good strategy, because it can lead to ruminating about the issue and the person and to feelings of resentment and hostility that go beyond the issue. Additionally, refusing to speak for long periods of time, or not at all, about a problem leaves an *open wound* that may never heal properly. Unresolved conflicts never leave a relationship; they surface time and again, often affecting other parts of the relationship and ultimately causing it to spiral downward.

• Respect Each Other

When two people communicate, it is necessary that they act in a way that clearly indicates they respect each other and consider themselves to be equals. Respecting someone means that you think of them as a valuable and worthwhile person, and that what they have to say is worth listening to. It is an extremely important ingredient of all relationships but especially those that are more intimate, such as a marriage.

Respect can be conveyed by words, but also by our tone and body language. When we talk down to someone, it is generally interpreted by that person as a lack of respect and interferes in the communication process. It's not uncommon for someone who is being treated as an inferior to say, *I don't like your tone of voice.* The person being talked down to pays more attention to the negative attitude and can't focus as much as they need to on the messages being conveyed. The conversation becomes more about how something is said rather than what is being said. In that way a condescending tone can move a communication off its intended objective. Additionally, the person taking on a superior role is not likely to take information presented to them very seriously. It is hard to give attention and credence to something said by somebody who we think is beneath us.

Along with disrupting communication, treating someone as an inferior gets paid back in how they treat us in return. What we think about another person is affected by what we think he or she thinks about us. So when we're condescending, patronizing, or disrespectful in other ways, not only will a communication move in the wrong direction, but that person will think less well about us.

• Listen to Each Other

Sometimes couples get into the habit of talking *at* each other and not *to* each other. We call this a *mutual monologue.* If you've ever watched a political debate, you've watched a mutual monologue. Each candidate is interested only in saying what he or she has to say; they are not concerned with interacting and sharing ideas with each other. That is to say, each is talking but they are not communicating with each other.

Many married couples who have trouble resolving conflicts communicate in this way. A marriage counselor once was working with a couple that was having very severe marital problems. They had complicated their problems with extramarital affairs and all kinds of negativity. It attempting to determine how they communicated, the marriage counselor asked how often they talked. They said they spoke several times a day, often for a very long time. They described the *discussion* they had a few days prior, which lasted from four o'clock in the afternoon until three o'clock the next morning.

The marriage counselor carefully watched as each person talked. Each talked a lot about their own issues. The marriage counselor stopped the conversation at times and asked the spouse who was not talking what the other person had just said. Neither spouse could accurately report what the other said because they just weren't listening to what the other had to say.

Although it is important to talk when you communicate, only by listening to the other person can you avoid an ongoing mutual monologue. Communication includes conveying information about ourselves, but it also includes reacting and responding to the information conveyed to us. If we're not listening, we can't react, and we won't be able to take into account the thoughts and feelings of the other person. That means we can't come to solutions.

Careful listening is also a way that we can avoid misinterpretations. Very often a person can tell if their message was accurately received by the reaction to it. Of course, miscommunications will still happen from time to time. If that is a chronic problem in your relationship, you and your partner might find it useful to practice repeating back what the other partner said. In such exercises the emphasis must be on what *you* understood was said. Keep in mind what we mentioned earlier about information processing and how our perceptions affect our interpretation of what is communicated to us.

• Be Honest

Although we were all brought up hearing the old adage, *Honesty is the best policy*, at times it can be extremely difficult for human beings to tell the truth. This is particularly the case when the situation is uncomfortable or involves conflict. Under these circumstances each of us has probably lied to save ourselves from conflict or embarrassment. Although we know we will have to deal with the consequences of our lies in the future, we will often put off pain in the present in the hope that somehow magically the problem will go away. Of course we also know that the problem is not going away, but that doesn't stop us from hoping.

A problem with lying is that sometimes we get away with it. When lying works, we temporarily avoid something negative from happening, and that reinforces our willingness to try it again. However, once someone catches us in a lie, there's a very strong likelihood they won't trust anything else that we say. Needless to say, this is very destructive to communication and can eat away at the heart of any relationship, even to the point of causing its demise.

As hard as it might be, we need to try to be as truthful as we can in our intimate relationships. When confronted with a distasteful situation, we need to make a fundamental decision. Do we want the intense pain of a conflict that can be over with and resolved? Or do we want the slow, gnawing pain that having lied creates in most of us? Besides misleading the other person, when we lie we're likely to experience guilt, that debilitating and nonadaptive emotion. Remember that guilt is only useful as a means of getting our attention so that we can do something about the reason we feel guilty. Beyond this, guilt is useless and can be very destructive. Consequently, we're better off avoiding the destructiveness of guilt by being as honest and straightforward as we can. It will be tough, but it is worth the effort and much less risky to the future of any relationship.

Before we leave the topic of honesty, it is necessary to make one additional point. Sometimes people use honesty as a weapon to *beat up* others. Honesty used in this way can be brutal and destructive. It is necessary to be honest in a reasonable and sensitive way. For example, if your spouse has bad breath, you can tell them in more than one way. You might say, *You have bad breath and I can't stand it. Do something about it now.* Some obnoxious hand movements could be added to really dramatize your point. You certainly would be honest using this approach, but it's not hard to imagine the type of reaction your partner would have and how he or she might feel about you.

As an alternative, suppose you said, *Honey, I know that you try to keep your physical appearance as good as possible and you always look great. Lately, I have noticed that your breath is somewhat strong. Maybe you need to see your dentist or physician to see what the problem might be. I know this is hard for you to hear, but I am telling you this because I care about you and I know you would want to know this so that you could do something about it. I'll be glad to do whatever I can to help.*

These are two very honest statements that get the point across. However, they convey two very different messages and will produce very different effects on a relationship. While they both are likely to get someone with bad breath to deal with their problem, the former will also lead your partner to feel humiliated and not very happy with the relationship.

• Trust Each Other

Trust is considered to be one of the cornerstones of any close relationship. Its importance is demonstrated by the fact that a lack or breakdown of trust is usually a precursor to a relationship's demise. Some violations of trust, such as marital infidelity, can be devastating to a marriage because they are difficult, if not impossible, for many people to forgive.

We know there's trust in our relationships when we allow ourselves to be vulnerable. In doing so, we set up a potentially dangerous situation for ourselves because we provide others with an opportunity to hurt us if they choose to. However, we are willing to expose our innermost thoughts and feelings to others because we believe they won't hurt us or use what we confide in them against us.

Trust varies in degree; it is not all or none. It builds slowly in a relationship and is based on having a number of experiences in which the other person demonstrates a willingness to help and protect us. Trust also goes hand in hand with respect and they build on each other. Very often you learn to respect those persons whom you trust, and trust those persons whom you respect. The more consistently positive our experiences are with other people across a variety of situations, the more we will trust and respect them. We wouldn't be very wise if we immediately and completely trusted everyone that we met and knew because not everyone is trustworthy or has our best interests at heart.

It also would not be very wise or helpful if we never trusted anyone. When we don't trust others, we keep them at a distance and shut them out of our lives. We generally take that route as a form of self-preservation. We prevent them from getting close enough to hurt us. Unfortunately, this also prevents people from getting close enough to love and be intimate with us. We must certainly trust our friends, spouse, and members of our family if we are to have healthy and growing relationships with them.

Trust is essential for communicating with others. Without trust there can be no effective communication because we cannot be honest about our true thoughts and feelings. We won't be able to discuss certain issues because we fear how others might react or how they might think of us. As a result, we can't have our personal needs addressed and that makes it hard to feel emotionally connected to the relationship.

If you have a hard time trusting others, you need to understand the reasons why you think that way. Again, we would encourage you to use self-reflection to explore the beliefs that underlie the reasons. You might find, for example, that your lack of trust is tied to some past experiences in which others have harmed you. While it's rational to believe that those who have betrayed you should not be trusted, it is irrational to believe that all people cannot be trusted as a result. Being able to trust is so important to psychological health that if you cannot find what is at the core of your mistrusting on your own, it would be worthwhile to seek professional help to overcome this problem.

• Avoid Unanswerable Questions

When we communicate we often ask questions of each other. The type of question we ask can make a big difference to the outcome of our discussions. It's not often helpful to ask too many *why* questions. People are not often aware of why they did particular things until they think them through. The motivation for some behaviors is sometimes unconscious.

Asking questions that imply the answer or ones that do not have a real answer is also not helpful. If you ask, *Why don't you love me?* or, *Why is it that whenever I ask you to do something, you don't seem to take my requests seriously?* the other person won't know how to answer. We predict that what will follow these questions are arguments and fighting, and not much will be resolved.

Sentiments such as these are best addressed as statements rather than questions. You could say, *I think you don't love me because . . .* and then state your reasons. You might say, *I have asked you to do the following things on many occasions and I don't think you have done them. Can we discuss this?* These statements can lead to fruitful discussion and resolution. If you need to ask questions, it is best to ask factual questions that can be answered.

Sometimes when people say, *I don't know*, they are trying to avoid dealing with something that is unpleasant to them. However, sometimes they actually don't know. Nagging and pushing will not get them to know it any better. Repeating yourself over and over again also does not increase the likelihood that you will get an answer, nor does saying something louder and nastier make it any clearer. Instead, you end up raising the emotional bar, which often results in a response in kind.

- **Choose Words Carefully**

Sometimes when we're in the midst of a conflict we may say things we don't mean or are better left unsaid. It's an easy trap to fall into because emotions run high in such situations and we're less in control of ourselves. Nevertheless, insults, accusations, demands, threats, swearing, sarcasm, name calling, and all other forms of abusive language won't help the communication process. Such language expresses contempt. It also provokes anger and usually leads to counterpunches and hostile comebacks. Solutions to problems won't surface when conflicts go down this path.

Even if words are not abusive and the tone is respectful, there are other language issues that can interfere with communication. Accuracy of our statements is one. This includes a clear expression of our issue, but it also means to avoid hyperbole and exaggeration. A sentence that starts with the words, *You always . . .* is begging for a hostile response. When we tell a partner that they *always* do something wrong, they are compelled to point out the occasions when they did not do or say such things. That changes the conversation to a historical review of the relationship and starts the escalation process. Exaggerated statements are also likely to leave others feeling incompetent and without clear direction. How can they improve when they *always do or say the wrong things?*

Pronouns also affect our communication effectiveness in a conflict. *I, we,* and *you* convey very different messages and suggest what's really at the center of our thinking. The first person plural pronoun is often the better way to go. When we use *we,* partners imply that their identities are defined as a couple rather than as individuals. During a conflict, *we* also suggests that a problem is owned together and both are responsible for coming up with a solution. Couples have an easier time finding a solution that suits both of them when the problem is considered to be shared.

Using first person singular pronouns, such as *I* or *my*, are also acceptable when you're describing personal thoughts or feelings. Self-disclosure can be an important step in working through a problem. The information we provide about ourselves gives others something to think about and react to. They have a better idea where we're coming from and have a path for clearing up misunderstandings and disagreements.

However, *I* may not be the best way to start a conversation when it's linked to a negative idea, such as when sentences begin with *I don't like it when you* . . . A negatively worded statement doesn't say what we want from someone. It tells them what not to do but not what they should do instead. It's also accusatory and can provoke a hostile response. Setting up the statement in the positive, such as, *I would prefer that you* . . . provides your partner with direction as to what you want from them without directly accusing them of some wrongdoing.

You is the real problem pronoun during conflicts. Sentences that begin with *you* can easily cause disagreements to digress and escalate. That pronoun is often used to place blame on someone (e.g., *you do or don't do this*). It is also used when we claim to know someone's innermost thoughts and feelings (e.g., *you think or believe that*). Such accusations and attributions produce negative reactions because the accused has to defend their actions, and that can put them on the defensive or cause them to respond with their own accusations. Attributing thoughts and beliefs to your partner leaves them in the uncomfortable and frustrating position of trying to persuade the other that he or she really doesn't think or feel a certain way.

• Have the Right Attitude

Effective communication requires that we bring the right perspective, especially in conflict situations. For one, we should try to be accommodating, that is, be willing to bend and negotiate. When we approach conflicts with a mind toward reconciliation, we're more willing to make sacrifices or negotiate trade-offs so that both partners' needs are met. We also treat other people's issues seriously, make an effort to understand their concerns, and have less difficulty admitting when we're at fault.

On the other hand, if we're nonaccommodating, we focus more on our personal needs than the needs of the relationship, and that usually means negotiation is not part of the reconciliation process. Because we're focused on ourselves, we might try to browbeat the other person until our own personal goals are agreed to. However, if our spouse gives in to our demands, typically it's not without a price. They usually walk away from the experience with negative feelings about the relationship and may feel cheated because their own needs were not considered.

Other attitudes that go hand in hand with accommodation are empathy and open-mindedness. With empathy, we identify with our partner's issues and can walk in their shoes. That lets them feel their opinions are worthwhile and respected and will make them feel good about us and the relationship. Open-mindedness refers to being able to consider alternatives. We can acknowledge that while our personal point of view may hold merit, the same is true for our partner. When we approach disagreements with an open mind, we don't have preconceived expectations about the outcome. Consequently, we have a better chance of coming up with solutions that meet our needs and that of our partner.

Having the right attitude also includes a willingness to forgive. If your spouse admits to a wrongdoing and apologizes, accept the apology, and if not, offer to forgive it nonetheless. If you plan to stay in the relationship, there is no value whatsoever in holding onto anger or other bad feelings once you and your partner have resolved a conflict. Retained disappointments cloud how you think of your partner, and those thoughts will haunt your relationship well into the future. Of course, if it's the same problem that keeps emerging, an apology is meaningless and you haven't resolved the problem. However, barring often repeated offenses, you will do a lot of good for your marriage by letting bygones be bygones.

- **Make Time to Communicate**

It is important to make the commitment to work on your relationships, especially if you have problems communicating with other people. We repeat this point again here because we are aware that although people recognize the importance of communication for the health of a relationship, they don't always realize that to do it truly well requires practice. We know that if you don't plan to set aside the time to improve your communication skills, you won't. Too many things can get in the way and time slips away faster than we think. Besides, there is a lot that goes into effective communication. Trying to remember all the rules can be difficult, and only by putting in dedicated time and effort can they be learned well enough to become a habit.

An important point to remember is that when we use ineffective communication, we end up with negative outcomes. Ineffective communication prevents us from reaching solutions, tends to prolong arguments by sending us off the issue, and usually causes arguments to escalate out of proportion to the original problem. On the other hand, by following the principles we have laid out, you'll find your discussions are more productive and meaningful. Importantly, because you will work through your problems together, you will strengthen the emotional bond between you and your spouse.

On a final note, keep in mind that conflicts are not about winning. They're about maintaining and improving a relationship. When there's a winner, there's also a loser, and a loser never feels good about the experience. Truly effective communication not only leads to resolution but avoids escalation. In the end, each partner feels their point of view was heard and understood, so they feel good about each other and believe their relationship has moved in a positive direction.

SUMMARY

Communication is essential to good relationships as food and water are important for the health of a living body. There is a lot going on when we communicate with other people. Not only do we use different modes of communicating, but we also communicate different kinds of information, including our thoughts, beliefs, and emotions. Additionally, our interpretation of what is being communicated is affected by our own beliefs, thoughts, and values.

With such a complex process, it's not surprising that we may run into problems when we communicate with others. This can especially be the case when it comes to intimate relationships, particularly when couples are faced with conflict situations. We have outlined a number of points to keep in mind that can help you improve how you and your partner communicate with each other. It is important that you dedicate the time and effort to try to learn how to be an effective communicator so that conflicts are resolved quickly and your relationship can grow and flourish.

9

HANDLING DIFFICULT INTERACTIONS

Most of us dislike confrontation. When faced with difficult interpersonal interactions, we get uncomfortable and try to avoid them. Nevertheless, avoiding confrontations completely is impossible, especially with people we are close to. Just by nature of the amount of time spent together these relationships will have their fair share of conflicts.

As we discussed in the previous chapter, resolving conflicts quickly and relatively painlessly requires certain kinds of communication skills. However, even if we are quite adept at these skills, there are some relationships, or some conflicts in the best relationships, where our communication styles just don't seem to be effective. The reality is some people are difficult and some occasions are so emotion packed that basic communication skills are just not enough. It's in situations like these when you might feel your emotions get the better of you, and that means you won't be as in control of events and your life as you could be.

In this chapter, we focus on the thought processes and provide the tools that may help you deal with the more difficult kinds of interactions. Adopting some of these techniques will not only make you more effective in dealing with these situations. You might also find that they help you to feel more in control and may improve your relationships along the way.

Broadly speaking there are three types of interpersonal interactions: neutral, positive, and negative. These types of interactions are defined by the specifics of the situation in which they occur, as well as the types of emotions that are associated with them. In a neutral interaction, there is little emotional arousal and little emotional interaction. If you go to the grocery store and buy a loaf of bread, you would probably have a neutral interaction with the people you meet there. You choose the bread and give the cashier the money. He or she thanks you. You receive your change, thank the cashier, and leave. Most of our everyday interactions fall into the neutral category.

In positive interpersonal interactions, we experience positive human emotions, such as love, affection, gratitude, and respect. When you tell someone you love them, or praise them, you are involved in a positive interpersonal interaction. Many of us find such interactions to be a source of pleasure. Unfortunately, there are others who have difficulty with certain types of positive interactions. They might find it uncomfortable to show love, affection, or gratitude and find it equally or more difficult to accept expressions of love, praise, and admiration. It is interesting that some people find it easier to say *I love you* to someone else than to have another person say that to them. Nevertheless, most of us enjoy such interactions and go out of our way to seek them out.

Negative interpersonal interactions are accompanied by negative emotions and may occur with someone close to you or a complete stranger. Typically, they involve the experience of having someone violate your rights and intrude upon your personal boundaries or space. The degree to which negative interactions have an effect on us depends upon how important the situation is to us. The situation and context of a negative interaction also determines the type and the intensity of the emotions we experience. For example, we would react less negatively to someone cutting in front of us when waiting in a line than we would to our spouse accusing us of cheating on them.

When we experience someone violating our rights, we can react in one of four ways: passively, aggressively, passive-aggressively, or assertively. When we act passively, we appear to be saying and doing nothing. We say *appearing* because actually much is going on inside our heads. It is likely that we're experiencing anger and frustration and possibly ruminating about feeling violated, although none of this is apparent to those who are observing us.

When we act passively, we experience a lot of negative side effects. We will often feel angry at ourselves and others. It is likely that we may express our anger on others later on, but not to the person who we feel violated us. Because we take out our frustration on others, we can experience guilt and lowered self-confidence after the fact, and we might put ourselves down for not standing up for our rights. When we don't stand up for ourselves, we have surrendered personal control of our emotions and behavior to the violator. When we do that we increase our negative self-assessment and thoughts of helplessness.

Another way we can react in this type of situation is aggressively, either overtly or passively. When we are openly aggressive, we attack others, either verbally or physically. Raising your voice or making threatening and angry gestures are examples of aggressive responses. Openly aggressive behavior is easily observed by others. When we act passive-aggressively, we appear to be passive but express our anger in indirect ways. We might rely on sarcasm or other indirect gestures to let others know that we are angry without addressing them directly. Passive-aggressive behavior comes in many forms, including sarcasm, procrastination, chronic lateness, blaming others for mistakes, giving the silent treatment, and purposely being vague, among others.

Although acting passively and openly aggressive appears to be very different, they often put us in the same undesirable situation. When we attack someone, we might think we have taken back control, but in fact the reverse happens. We lose whatever control we could have exercised over ourselves and the situation. We often find ourselves experiencing unproductive emotions, such as guilt, anger, and frustration. That means we give up responsibility and control over our behavior and that can lead to us blaming others for our emotions and behaviors. We also tend to switch our focus away from the situation and onto the person we are attacking. From the opposite perspective, the person we attack tends to solidify his or her position and that makes it difficult for them to change their behavior.

As an alternative approach, you could act assertively. When you are assertive, you address people directly in a polite and reasonable manner and point out to them how you believe they have violated your rights. In effect, you are asking them to take responsibility for their own behavior and change the situation. Acting assertively can often lead us to have positive thoughts about ourselves because we have maintained our self-respect and behaved respectfully to others. At the same time, we have taken reasonable action to prevent others from violating our rights.

We must emphasize that assertiveness is not about being patient and nice, although it may appear that way. It's about standing up for your rights, but doing so in a more productive and less belligerent manner, one that leaves you feeling in control and better about yourself. As an important point about assertiveness, you're not likely to have a negative interaction and question whether or not you behaved in an acceptable manner, you won't hold onto negative thoughts to ruminate over, and you won't feel a need to express your negative emotions inappropriately on others.

Assertiveness can be an excellent technique for dealing with most people. However, not all people we come into contact with are reasonable or considerate. When confronted by individuals who are particularly difficult, we might have to use more than just assertive language to protect our rights. Additional action on our part might be called for, that is, we have to escalate our response. Very often we think of escalation as aggressiveness, either in the form of words or actions, but that's not what we mean. Escalation involves being stronger, contacting an authority, or removing ourselves from the situation. It does not mean getting angry or behaving in an abusive manner. Such an approach is never a good idea because it prevents us from feeling in control of the situation and leaves us feeling less effective and less positive about ourselves.

The choice of action depends on which one you believe is most appropriate at that time. For example, suppose you go to visit your physician and are sitting in the waiting room where there is a large sign that clearly indicates that smoking is not allowed. Also, suppose a large man enters the room smoking a cigar. He sits down next to you and continues to smoke his cigar, apparently ignoring the sign. How would you respond?

You could sit there and do nothing, that is, you can be passive. It is likely that you would be talking to yourself in a very angry tone. You would probably be telling yourself that he is a rude and inconsiderate person who doesn't care about you or others. You might even hope that someone else would say something to him, but nothing happens. Later on, after you leave the office, you would still be angry and you might even displace that anger on others, perhaps through impatience or hostile language.

Another way to react to this situation would be to be aggressive. You could yell at the man and tell him how rude and inconsiderate he is. You might even threaten him and insist that he put out his damn cigar. You could also be passive-aggressive. You might start coughing aloud and waving your hand in the air to push the smoke away from you. You might talk in a low voice, loud enough so that he could hear you, and let him know what you think about people who ignore others. You would never address him directly, but you would be sure he got your message.

Finally, you could be assertive. You might say, *Excuse me sir, the smoke from your cigar is bothering me. I would appreciate it if you could do something about it.* If he says he has the right to smoke, you might point out to him politely the sign that indicates that he does not have the right to smoke in that room.

When we are assertive, we don't attack people or allow ourselves to become angry, or experience other emotions that cause us to lose control of the situation. We don't do to them what we believe they are doing to us. We separate them from their behavior and allow them the opportunity to acknowledge our request and make a reasonable response to it.

Here is what we would suggest you do if the person doesn't comply with your request. Suppose the person says that he doesn't care about the sign and he plans to continue to smoke. When you are assertive you know you have done what you can do to resolve the situation reasonably. Your next step is to escalate. You could go to the receptionist and ask her to intervene. If this fails, you could wait until you see the physician and tell him what happened. If he fails to handle the situation, your primary option is to move away from the smoker, and then it may be time to find another physician.

The point is an assertive reaction allows us to stay in control. We won't hold anger inside of us and express it in inappropriate ways that could lead us to feel bad about ourselves, as we would if we took a passive approach. We also won't act out our anger or express other hostile emotions either actively or passively, which could lead us to feel guilty, as we would if we took an aggressive approach. Instead, by acting assertively, we can maintain our own composure, and at the same time we maximize the likelihood the other person will act reasonably and appropriately. In acting assertively, we take responsibility for our behavior and ask the other person to take responsibility for her or his behavior.

Assertive behavior also allows us to avoid putting ourselves in the position of doing something we might regret later. This can happen when we incorrectly assess a situation and believe that someone has violated our rights. For example, suppose we were waiting in line for a movie and thought that a person cut in line in front of us. Suppose also, that this person had actually not done that. If we have acted aggressively or passive-aggressively, we would find ourselves in an embarrassing situation because we acted out inappropriately. If we acted passively, we would have spent a great deal of needless effort being angry at that person and ourselves.

Acting assertively, on the other hand, puts us in a much better position. For one, we have taken responsibility for our thoughts and feelings and have not assumed that what we perceived was correct. We did not allow our misperceptions to get the better of us, and we didn't waste our time and energy over a violation of our rights that didn't happen. We also don't have to speculate whether the person would have been cooperative if we had approached him more appropriately. If the other person won't be cooperative when we are assertive, it is likely they won't be cooperative no matter what else we do. In fact, they may have a much worse response if they're confronted aggressively.

Being assertive allows us to graciously back off the situation because we have not attacked anyone. If, in the above example, you assert yourself and then realize that the other person actually did not cut in line, you can apologize. Since you have not been impolite or aggressive, you have nothing to be regretful for. Human beings make mistakes and the best we can do is learn from those mistakes and apologize. However, if the other person gets angry at your mistake, then you might need to handle that new situation assertively.

Assertiveness is also the best way to handle people who we believe are trying to manipulate or control us. Many of us have had people in our lives who have tried to get us to do things we don't want to do. We are not talking about authority figures, such as your boss, your parents, or a teacher, but rather people who have no direct authority over you. As we have stated numerous times, just as it is unwise (and impossible) to try to control others, the same is true for allowing others to control you.

When other people try to control us, they are taking the responsibility for our life out of our hands and into their own. If we allow that to happen, the decisions they make for us are in their interests and not necessarily ours, but we are the ones who have to live with these decisions. We may also find it difficult to come up with workable plans to reach goals because they're somebody else's goals, not our own. When we let someone else control us, we may develop a sense of helplessness in the face of problems because we have less experience in handling them ourselves. So while it may appear to be the easier path to let others make decisions for us, over the long term it actually makes our life more difficult.

How do you handle a person who is trying to take control of your life? Suppose someone tells you that you must do something or act in a certain way that you reject. A passive-aggressive response might be to follow their direction—or act like you plan to—but then procrastinate in getting it done. You might feel angry or helpless because you're not sure how to proceed. If you behave aggressively, you might show your anger and say something like, *Don't tell me what to do!* Again, afterward you might feel bad or guilty about your reaction.

An assertive response, in contrast, might include explaining why you have made the decision to do what you want and then adding something like, *I am the one who has to live with this decision, so I want to do what I believe is best for me.* You will be in control of yourself, yet you won't feel angry or regret having said something that was hurtful or insulting. We should try to keep in mind that people who try to manipulate us very often believe they have our best interests at heart. In other words, they may actually care about us, despite the fact that their attentiveness is expressed inappropriately. Acting assertively means we won't behave in ways that would hurt their feelings and possibly damage the relationship.

COMPONENTS OF AN ASSERTIVE RESPONSE

There are actually some very specific and definable components that make up assertive behavior. These components include the following:

1. Assertive responses are consistent. As we discussed in the previous chapter, we not only communicate to others by the content of what we say but also by our eye contact, body posture, gestures, facial expressions, the distance between us and the other person, along with our tone of voice, inflection, and volume. In being assertive, look the other person directly in the eyes, stand erect, make sure your voice is clear and distinct and at an appropriate volume. Make sure the inflection in your voice reflects the message you want to give and make sure your gestures go with your words.

No matter how well you construct the content of your assertive response, if you hunch over, look to the floor, put your hands in your pockets, or talk in a low monotone voice, you will come across as passive and not assertive. Conversely, if you get too close to the other person, wave your arms in a menacing way, raise your voice, and use a harsh tone, you will be perceived as overly aggressive no matter what you say.

2. An assertive response sends the message to the recipient that we are taking responsibility for our behavior and emotions. It also communicates clearly that we expect the other person to take responsibility for his or her behavior and emotions. All of this is done without the use of threats or other hostile language.

3. Assertive messages focus on the *behavior* that we find intrusive or offensive, not the *person*, and are not hostile or abusive. Here is an example that highlights the difference between assertive and aggressive responding. Assume once again that you are in a situation in which smoking is not allowed and someone is smoking. An aggressive response might be, *You are making me sick with your cigarette smoke. Put the damn thing out NOW or else I'll call the police.* If you wanted to be assertive you might instead say, *Excuse me, I'm not sure whether you are aware that smoking is not permitted here. Also, the smoke from your cigarette is making me nauseous and I would appreciate it if you could put your cigarette out. Thank you.*

4. An assertive response offers the other person choices. You do not try to force a particular course of action on another person, but instead let them decide for themselves what they want to do. In each of the examples of assertive responses we've presented, the other person is offered responses that will resolve the conflict. Most people are willing to be compliant with a request that is reasonable and presented in an assertive yet nonhostile manner. If they are not, you

need to consider escalating the interaction as we described previously.

PRACTICING YOUR ASSERTIVE RESPONSE

Although these rules are simple and straightforward, it is not always easy to act assertively. In a confrontation we can get caught up in the moment. It is not unusual for people to take on an aggressive tone or demeanor in conflict situations and not realize they are acting that way. This lack of awareness is most likely to occur if the actual words being used are not aggressive. When we use abusive or hostile words, we know full well that we are behaving aggressively. However, when we use words that seem courteous, we can sometimes fool ourselves into thinking we are behaving calmly and appropriately, but our demeanor will likely convey aggressiveness.

We may also not know how we should appear when we're being assertive so that it's clear we are acting assertively to another person. For this reason, it is a wise idea to practice assertiveness by rehearsing imaginary interactions. Using a mirror and/or a tape recorder can help you develop an assertive style that works for you. It can also be helpful to watch an assertive model and analyze what he or she has done. This will often widen your options and let you learn what we need to learn.

To become truly proficient at assertiveness, try to plan your responses when you can and analyze what you did after you have acted. The more we analyze our own behavior, the more we know about ourselves. The more we know about ourselves, the more control we will have over our own behavior. Consequently, we can act the way we want and not let circumstances control us. Monitoring your behavior is another form of self-reflection, and as we've said many times, nothing beats self-reflection for understanding who you are.

POSSIBLE NEGATIVE REACTIONS TO ASSERTIVENESS

Unfortunately, as we have already pointed out, despite the best efforts and most detailed planning, some people will still react negatively when we are assertive. In the face of reasonableness, they may react aggressively toward us, or they may overapologize, or they may attempt to deny any wrongdoing. Some people might even regard assertive talk as patronizing and dismiss it as disrespectful or denigrating.

If that happens to you, it is best not to confront the other person about their reaction but to keep acting assertively and not allow yourself to act passively, aggressively, or passive-aggressively. If a person gets aggressive or threatens violence, it may be necessary to be more forceful in your response by getting tougher, without aggressiveness, or bringing in outside help. Note, however, that sometimes leaving the situation is the best solution. If you try being assertive and the other person refuses to be cooperative, you won't feel angry later if you leave.

CHOOSING NOT TO ASSERT YOURSELF

There are situations and circumstances where it is not always necessary to act assertively. For example, you may find it best not to assert yourself with someone who is overly sensitive. Of course, it is possible that this person has learned to act in an overly sensitive manner in order to get what he or she wants. You might also choose not to assert yourself if you believe that the other person is under unusual duress and that your assertiveness would be an undue burden for them. Of course, if this is the other person's usual state, it sometimes can be best to leave the relationship, or at least limit your interactions with them. However, if the other person's behavior is atypical for them, you might let it go and give them the benefit of the doubt. Good friends deserve a break. As the old saying goes, *Treat others as you would have them treat you.*

You could also decide not to be assertive if the person recognizes that his or her behavior is violating your rights and is aware of the need to act differently or apologize. Being assertive in this case is really being aggressive. Again, treat others as you would want to be treated. The point for each of these situations is that you focus on maintaining control of your behavior. The choice is yours. It isn't useful to be a slave to anyone or anything, including assertiveness.

SUMMARY

As much as we might find them distasteful, we cannot completely avoid conflicts and difficult situations with other people. When faced with confrontation and we feel our rights have been violated, we can either act passively, aggressively, or assertively. Of these, assertiveness is the best way to react when you believe someone has violated your rights. When we react passively or aggressively, we tend to lose control over ourselves and the situation, and we are likely to experience unproductive emotions, such as guilt, anger, and frustration. Acting assertively, on the other hand, allows us to stay in control and feel good about ourselves while preventing others from controlling us.

There are certain principles to follow in order to become more assertive, and we've outlined these principles so you have a game plan to follow. However, it takes more than knowing the rules to develop an assertive style. You need to make a commitment to changing, observe and learn from your own behavior, plan and practice your assertiveness, observe yourself trying to be assertive, change your response as needed, and keep working at it. Remember, thoughtful practice will make you better at anything, including how you interact with others.

10

DEVELOPING AND FINE-TUNING YOUR SKILLS

Throughout the previous chapters we've presented a number of principles and guidelines to help you adjust your way of thinking so that you can improve how you handle people and situations and thereby gain greater control over your life. The purpose of this chapter is to provide a summary of the particularly salient ideas, along with exercises that will help you achieve that goal. As we've stressed throughout, it takes a good deal of effort and concentration to break old habits. You have to identify the irrational beliefs that drive inappropriate and damaging emotions, and then learn to adjust those beliefs.

As you work through the exercises presented below, you will probably find you need to go back and read the relevant chapters again. There you will find more detail and true to life examples that can strengthen your learning. Rereading and reviewing will be worth the effort because you will find that you can use many of these ideas and methods to handle a variety of issues in your life.

SELF-REFLECTION

Here is where it all starts. Because thoughts and beliefs are considered to be the underlying causes of human emotions and behavior, the most important tool we have at our disposal for identifying those beliefs is self-reflection. There are many events and commitments that take place each day of our lives that trigger a range of thoughts, emotions, and actions. Getting better control over our lives requires that we spend some time alone each day reviewing these events and examining the thoughts and feelings that went along with them. It is important to make a commitment to take the time each day to spend some time with yourself.

Taking time for ourselves is an essential ingredient for maintaining our emotional well-being and growing our relationships. A psychologically healthy life requires that you learn to live *with* yourself, not *by* yourself. The more you get to know yourself by examining your own values, thoughts, and beliefs, the better off you will be as a person and the better off your marriage and other relationships will be.

Exercise

To get started, we recommend that you obtain a recording device. In the era of smartphones, this should not require much effort or cost. It is also wise to buy yourself a notebook. You can use an electronic device (tablet or computer), but make sure you can carry that device with you. Plan to be in a private place by yourself for no more than fifteen to thirty minutes. In your notebook, make a short list of events or issues that have happened in your life that you want to review. These events could be positive, negative, or neutral. Instead of just thinking to yourself about these issues, speak your thoughts out loud and record them.

After you have recorded your thoughts and emotions about an event, play the recording back and make some notes. Your notes should include an analysis of your thinking, that is, the factors that led to the thoughts and emotions you experienced. Specifically, you should be looking for both rational and irrational beliefs that are underneath your thoughts and emotions. If you're having trouble with identifying these, you might want to refer to the table we provided in chapter 6 as a starting place. While these might trigger your thinking process, over time it is best to compile your own list of personal beliefs. Irrational beliefs come in all forms and have varied content, and you're likely to have a few we haven't included and that apply just to you.

As you accumulate your list of rational and irrational beliefs from your verbalizations, look for recurring themes, that is, the same emotions or thoughts that emerged in different situations. This will give you a good idea of the issues that are especially important for you. In doing your review, be sure to note the irrational beliefs and write out countering rational beliefs as is shown in table 6.1. Review your notes and your analysis as many times as you can. Try to do this exercise no less than three times a week, but more frequently if you have the time. The more you do it, the more you will become aware of the thoughts and beliefs that are behind your emotions.

MAKING THE UNCONSCIOUS CONSCIOUS

The unconscious-irrational level of functioning has the characteristics opposite to those of the conscious-rational level of functioning. Unconscious thoughts and beliefs do not follow the rules of logic and reason, and they are uninfluenced by time. The distinction between past, present, and future becomes unclear, and instead, the greatest emphasis is on the here and now. According to Freud, functioning at this level is characterized by an irrational drive to immediately satisfy needs and reduce discomfort.

The unconscious-irrational level of functioning is where irrational beliefs reside. The fact that the two types of beliefs, rational and irrational, reside in different levels of human functioning can be used to explain why people can hold both types of beliefs about the same issue at the same time. It also can be used to explain why human thinking and behavior is not always clearly understandable and predictable, since a rational or irrational belief can be dominant at different times, and because irrationality has an illogical and unpredictable nature.

Exercise

Unconscious thinking is most likely to emerge when we are reacting to negative events. Pick a recent negative event that you have experienced. This might be a disagreement you had with someone or some event you lived through that left you feeling angry or frustrated (e.g., being turned down for a job you wanted, being rejected by a person you wanted to date, losing some valuable object, getting stuck in traffic, etc.). After turning on your recording device, review that event in your head and say everything that comes to mind no matter how it may sound to you as you say it out loud.

Using your notes and the list of irrational thoughts you generated from your self-reflection exercise, analyze what you have said and see if you can identify which statements indicate unconscious thoughts and beliefs. Let's say you became angry because you were stuck in traffic. You might have to do some digging in your mind to come up with the unconscious thoughts that occurred at the time and led to your anger. These might include, *people don't know how to drive, there's no reason for this traffic,* or, *why does this always happen to me?* You know these thoughts are irrational because people do know how to drive, traffic tie-ups happen all the time for many reasons, and this is not happening specifically *to you,* it just happens. These are all beyond your control so they are irrational beliefs, and getting angry is nonadaptive and only ruins your day.

Not all unconscious thoughts and beliefs will surface easily the first time you perform this exercise. In fact, it will likely take many attempts and a lot of practice to develop an expertise for this skill. Nevertheless, if you work at it consistently, you will uncover more and more of your unconscious thoughts and beliefs. As you get better at it, then you can address these issues and come to a better understanding as to how they affect your emotions and behaviors.

CHANGING YOUR BEHAVIOR

Learning to have increased control over your life involves knowing how to make changes in your behavior. In order to make changes, we must first identify things that we want to change. It is important that we focus on those behaviors that are changeable and make sure we devise a plan that is feasible and reasonable.

There are a few points to keep in mind when we try to change how we behave. First, we must remember that habits are well-ingrained patterns of behaviors that have been woven into the fabric of our every-day lives, which makes them very difficult to change. Additionally, re-member that change follows a sawtooth curve of ups and downs, steps forward and steps backward. So be patient and keep in mind that it will take time and repeated attempts to reach your goal.

It is also important for us to remember that changing behavior will involve changing our beliefs. Consequently, our primary focus should be on uncovering our irrational beliefs through self-reflection before we try to change a behavior. Finally, keep in mind that it is unlikely that we will be able to change others. So if your behavior is a result of how someone else acts toward you, focus on changing how you react to that person rather than trying to change that person.

Exercise

Pick a behavior that you wish to change. For your first time, pick something simple. For example, you might choose regularly brushing your teeth in the morning and evening if that is something you wish to change. Any similar behavior will do. Once you pick a behavior, keep track of what you do now. Trying to change some behavior requires that we carefully keep a record of our progress. Again, we also need to understand that progress will be an up and down process. There may be times when you will slide back to your old patterns. It's normal if you do, so just stick with your plan and your goal.

Using your notebook, make a table listing the days of the week as the rows and morning and evening as the columns, just as shown in table 10.1

For each day, put a check mark each time you brush your teeth for the morning and evening. For each time you do not brush your teeth, write down the thoughts you have in your notebook, including the reasons why you did not do it. You might also want to record your thoughts using your recording device before you write them down. This exercise

Table 10.1. Charting a Behavior

	Morning	Evening
Monday		
Tuesday		
Wednesday		
Thursday		
Friday		
Saturday		
Sunday		

will tell you what thoughts went through your mind that might have prevented you from doing something you think you wanted to do. That will help you identify your irrational beliefs and work on counters to them.

Please note that just keeping a record of a behavior can cause it to change. Many years ago there was a program to help people stop cigarette smoking called Smokenders. The first step in this program was tracking smoking by writing down when you smoked a cigarette along with what conditions surrounded that event. Smokers found that just the act of recording each cigarette they smoked led them to smoke fewer cigarettes initially. However, over time, they found that they returned to their original smoking patterns unless they did something else to quit smoking.

If you are going to achieve real change, you have to get past the point where just by recording it there is a short-term change in that behavior. So before working on the actual behavior you want to change, it is important to monitor that behavior for some time before you try to change. Perhaps two or three weeks should be sufficient.

After the initial or baseline monitoring period is over, you need to introduce an intervention that will help you increase or decrease the behavior that you wish to change. You might reward yourself after each behavior or number of behaviors. You might allow yourself to watch a television show you like or do something else for yourself that you find pleasant. Be careful not to use something as a reward that is harmful to you. For example, if you also have a drinking problem, using alcohol as a reward may not be the best idea. Along these lines, you also wouldn't want to use sweets or other unhealthy foods as a reward if you have a problem controlling your weight.

Before you introduce the reward, you need to set a realistic goal of behavior change. Again, anticipate that your progress will follow an up and down curve rather than a straight line. You will take a step or two forward and a step or two backward as you strive toward your goal. At some point you can give up recording your behavior, but you might want to put that step back in if you feel yourself slipping.

Throughout the process it is necessary to monitor and analyze your thinking and work on countering the irrational beliefs (e.g., it is too hard to do this every day) that tend to sabotage your change. It is also important to avoid the search for magical solutions: that you will change your behavior without much effort. Magical solutions don't work and looking to them leads to disappointment, failure, and a waste of your valuable resources.

IMPROVING YOUR RELATIONSHIPS

Human beings are social animals. We live in communities and have a variety of social relationships, and the quality of these relationships is essential for our psychological health. Many of these relationships are formed and perpetuated by intention, such as with friends, a marriage partner, and other people in our social circle. However, some relationships exist without our intention or control. We don't choose our family members or many people who influence our lives (teachers, neighbors, authority figures, etc.).

For some of our relationships, either intentional or not, we might from time to time run into difficulties, or we might feel that they are just not as fulfilling as we would like them to be. Part of getting better control over our lives is to understand our relationships and making decisions about how to interact with others so that we find them more satisfying. Putting in the effort to improve such relationships is better than the alternatives, which might include keeping them in their present form (which is not to your liking), or dropping the relationships altogether without ever trying to improve them. If you try to fix things and they still don't work out for you, at least you will have fewer regrets.

Exercise

Pick a relationship you want to understand better or improve its quality. To start out, it might be wise to pick a relationship which is not central to your life. You might pick a coworker, a casual friend, or some other nonessential relationship. It's again time to take out your notebook and do some writing.

For this relationship, you need to identify the terms of your contract. List your rights and responsibilities and the other person's rights and responsibilities. For example, if the relationship is with a friend, your rights might include being allowed to request time together, to seek advice on a personal matter, to ask for help in doing something, and so on. Your responsibilities might include the same issues for your friend as they are for you. This list of rights and responsibilities spells out the details of your interpersonal contract with that person.

In making this list, you may discover there are inequalities in the rights and responsibilities for both parties that you were previously unaware of. You might find that you are primarily responsible for making plans to get together and that you are the one who always initiates contact; you are often doing favors for this person but they rarely do any for you; they confide in you but you rarely confide in them. The lopsidedness of the list may be the reason you might feel the relationship is uncomfortable and have come to the conclusion it needs to be changed.

Using this list, you can then plan a discussion with this friend to discuss your thoughts. This discussion is likely to reveal some of the unconscious aspects of your interpersonal relationship. These unconscious aspects are likely to be the source of the problems you have with this person. For example, you may discover that this person primarily wants to keep a relationship with you because of the things you do for him or her. Or you may have to admit to yourself that you don't confide in this person because you do not trust them. Note that being honest with yourself about who is doing what is essential to identifying and then fixing problems.

During that discussion you can try to renegotiate your contract. You can discuss the specific things that each of you can do to have a closer relationship. This negotiation will reveal the true nature of your relationship and may lead to its improvement. However, be prepared for the opposite result. This person may want the relationship to continue in its current unequal form and may be unwilling to make the changes you want. At that point you can decide whether it is in your interests to keep the relationship going, albeit with lower expectations as to what you will get out of it, lessen the value you give to this relationship, or gradually end it.

Throughout the process of trying to restructure your contract, keep in mind that it is a negotiation. You should be prepared to give things to this person that he or she wants in return for this person giving things to you. Additionally, the negotiation process requires that you keep an open mind and be willing to listen to this person's perceptions and feelings about the relationship. They may have legitimate reasons for their behavior, and you have to acknowledge such if you are going to move the relationship in the right direction.

IMPROVING YOUR COMMUNICATION

Understanding and analyzing communication is critical for human relationships. It is a highly complex process that is made up of many aspects or modes of human information transmission, including spoken language, nonverbal body language, facial expressions, as well as tone of voice and hand gestures. Every time we communicate with someone, we provide them with a great deal of information and they do the same for us. We transmit and receive facts, of course, but each party also conveys thoughts, emotions, and beliefs. Additionally, the messages we send out and receive are not just simply taken in; they are processed by our brains and are affected by our experiences, motivations, expectations, and memories. Remember that we often see what we expect to see and what we are used to seeing.

There is a particularly special relationship between emotions and perception. Negative emotions such as anger and anxiety *narrow* perception and prevent us from taking in all of the information available in our environment. This narrowing effect makes it difficult to process information accurately and as a result can have an adverse effect on our interpretation of what is being communicated. That is why it is better not to try to solve problems or engage in any very difficult task when you are highly emotionally aroused.

Effective communication is a two-directional act. Two people treat each other as equals, both are willing to listen, both are trying to be as constructively honest as possible, and both trust and respect each other. While communicating, it is wise to watch your emotional interference, avoid unanswerable questions, choose you words carefully, and stay on the issue. Given the complexities of the process and the problem that can arise when it's not done well, we suggest that you pick a place and time to communicate, especially if it is expected to be confrontational, when there is little or no interference.

Exercise

To improve your communication skills, start with spending some time thinking about your communication with those people with whom you regularly interact. Pick a situation in which you believe that the communication was ineffective and led to negative consequences. Write as much about this situation as you can remember. Review your notes and see if you can identify the issues that made the communication ineffective. As with other exercises, it is good to first talk out loud and record your verbalizations and then make notes.

After you believe you have identified the relevant issues, plan another communication with this person. Your goal is to address the issues that made the original communication ineffective. You might start the new communication by addressing what was said or done by you, or what was said or done to you, which you believe negatively impacted on the original communication.

Be sure not to blame the other person for his or her behavior, but emphasize the fact that these are things you perceived. Also point out that you would like to understand their perceptions of your communication, that is, how they interpreted what you said or did. Keep what you learned from this discussion in mind when you communicate with this person in the future. For example, you might find that a communication problem with this person often involves misinterpretation, or you or the other person might feel that the tonality of your typical conversation is hostile. You can then take precautions to avoid these same problems in your upcoming conversations. You should also review your future communications with this person to monitor whether or not they are progressing in a positive direction.

You can use a similar approach with your spouse for dealing with communication problems during conflicts. Choose a time when your relationship is calm. Ask your spouse if together you can come up with a better way of handling your conflicts so that they don't escalate into more intense battles. Approach the conversation by focusing on your partnership. You might try saying, *We should try to work on how we communicate when we argue.* Here the emphasis is on *we;* that will convey that you realize you and your spouse own the problem together.

Use your notes that you've put together as to what you perceive to be the issues that interfere with effective communication. Alternatively, you can write down your issues together. Discuss your own issues with your spouse, but also ask your spouse about his or her issues. You might also consider reading the chapter on communication together to uncover other problems that often seem to emerge during your conversations.

When you face a conflict in the future, keep in mind the decisions both of you have agreed to for communicating more effectively. Again, be aware that your styles might not change much in the first few encounters, but keep up the postreviewing and analysis process and eventually your styles will improve.

LEARNING TO BE MORE ASSERTIVE

Our interactions with others can be classified as positive, neutral, or negative. Of these, negative interactions can be the most difficult. These are interactions in which another person has violated our rights and intruded upon our personal space. When difficult interactions occur, these are often accompanied by negative emotions, and these can lead us to behave in inappropriate ways.

When we run into difficult interactions, we can react in one of four ways: passively, aggressively, passive-aggressively, or assertively. Of these, assertiveness is by far the most effective approach. Acting assertively produces positive feelings because we have maintained respect for ourselves and the other person, but we have also taken reasonable action to prevent others from violating our rights. We also maintain control of ourselves and the situation and don't allow negative emotions to take control of us.

Assertive responses are consistent, give the message that we are taking responsibility for our behavior and feelings, communicate clearly that we expect the other person to take responsibility for his or her actions, separate the behavior from the person, and offer the other person choices. When you are assertive, you address people directly in a polite and reasonable manner and point out how you believe they have violated your rights.

Exercise

It is usually best to start by picking a negative interaction in which you believe that you did not act in an appropriately assertive manner, that is, you were either aggressive or passive-aggressive. Again, talk aloud into your recording device about the situation, providing as much detail as possible. Try to analyze this situation using the principles on assertiveness outlined in chapter 9. Be sure to pay attention to the emotional content, your thoughts and beliefs, and your behaviors (actions) in this situation. Make detailed notes and review both the recording and your notes.

Once you've recorded what actually happened, the next stage is to write up what you would have liked your response to be if you could relive this situation. If possible, have the interaction again and see what happens, keeping in mind the principles we have outlined on assertive behavior. If that's not possible, note a similar situation and, using the method above, analyze your reaction to it and compare your notes from both interactions. What have you learned? What changed? What didn't? What might you do next time to be more assertive?

LEARNING TO FORGIVE

As we pointed out above, it is likely that some people will do things to us that we consider harmful. It is not uncommon for people to become insulted, hurt, angry, or have other similar reactions to a perceived harm. Sometimes we have a hard time forgetting the harm that we experienced. We might be thinking, *How could this person have done this to me? What's wrong with him or her? What's wrong with me?* This easily translates to . . . *This person should not have done this,* and, *if they did this, they must be bad, or I must be bad.*

As difficult as it might be at times, the path to psychological well-being and personal growth includes learning how to forgive. Holding a grudge will lead us to ruminate about these perceived hurts. Ruminating will not solve any problems and will lead to repeated episodes of negative emotions and perhaps even behavioral outbursts. Remember that ruminating has at its roots basic irrational beliefs. In the above example, notice the *shoulds* and *musts*, the hallmark of irrational beliefs. Forgiving, on the other hand, allows us to put past events in the past and minimizes the amount of time we waste by ruminating about these events.

Exercise

It is best to pick a recent situation that is not too highly emotionally charged, since these are generally easier for you to cope with. As you think about this situation, speak your thoughts out loud, writing them down and recording your speech. Take as much time as you need and try to say everything that you usually would say to yourself. After you've finished, play back your recording and listen carefully for irrational thoughts. Make notes about what you said and what you observed.

Review these notes and the recording as often as you can. You will notice a few things. First, you will hear your irrational beliefs (e.g., *He shouldn't have done that to me. She is a bad person for hurting my feelings*). Second, you will probably notice how many times you repeat the same thing and how much time your rumination takes up. This repetition is at the heart of rumination and is the major source of negative emotions.

The next step is to devise rational beliefs that counter these irrational beliefs. Every time you think an irrational thought, replace it with a rational one. Next, try to stop your train of thought by using tough self-talk. You might say to yourself, *Stop thinking about this NOW*. Another phrase that may help is, *I don't like feeling this way, so it's better for me to stop thinking this way*. This exercise has to be repeated often, since doing it only once or twice is not likely to have much effect. Feeling hurt and angry comes from a lot of practice, and changing it will take a lot of time and repetition.

The more difficult, long-term situations (e.g., being rejected by a parent, a divorce, a betrayal by someone you love) are much harder to get over and you may never put them away completely. The reality is you may never feel good about these situations. Nevertheless, the more you practice the more you will lessen their impact.

Forgiveness means moving on from hurts, lessening their impact, and spending less time focusing on negatives. Furthermore, remember that forgiveness is something you do for *yourself*, not for the person who has wronged you. When you forgive, you can reduce the negative emotions you experience and which can prevent you from feeling in control of your life.

DECISION MAKING

Although we have not addressed this topic formally, decision making can be difficult for many people. It is very common for patients to tell their therapist that they need to make a decision about some issue and just can't seem to do so. Problems with making decisions are another means by which we can feel helpless and not in control of our lives.

What makes decision making so hard? There seems to be two major obstacles. For one, people don't have a logical process to follow for making decisions; secondly, people can hold irrational beliefs about making decisions. To address the first issue of a logical process, outlined below is a step-by-step method that is actually attributed to Benjamin Franklin.

1. Clearly define the issue that needs a decision. Write the issue down in your notebook. Suppose you are unhappy and after some self-reflection decide that the reason you are making yourself unhappy has to do with your job. You can define the issue about which you wish to make decision as, *What will I do about my dissatisfaction with my job?*

2. List as many alternative solutions to this issue as you can. As you do, keep the following in mind:

- Be as creative as you can, even to the point of listing things that may seem absurd. This will give you some perspective as to the possible things that can be done. For example, in listing choices about what to do about your job you might include doing nothing, quitting your job right away, staying in bed for a week and not showing up for work, moving to Brazil, and so on.
- All choices will have positive and negative consequences. For example, if your choice is to quit your job, you will remove the source of your unhappiness (positive), but you will lose the income and enjoyable social relationships (negative) that you get from the job.
- There are no perfect choices, that is, there are no choices that do not have negative consequences. In fact, if there is one perfect

choice, there really is no choice at all. If we asked you to choose between a gift card for $1 or a gift card for $1,000, what would you do? Chances are you would ask, *what's the catch?* That's because you would realize the choices you've been given are too good to be true. So there must be a hidden agenda, or there really is no reasonable choice.

- Doing nothing is a choice and should be on the list. It also has positive and negative outcomes. In this case, doing nothing would mean staying at your job. The positive outcome would be you still have an income, and the negative outcome would be continued discontent.

- Many times a person can choose more than one alternative. However, some choices are irrevocable. You can do nothing for a while to see if you can make the situation better, while at the same time look for another job. However, if you quit immediately, that is an irrevocable choice and you must be prepared to live with both the positive and negative outcomes.

3. For each choice, list the possible positive and negative outcomes that choice will lead to. For each outcome, try to give a value to its importance. You can assign a number from 0 to 100 to each outcome, where 0 represents not at all important and 100 represents very important. For example, loss of income might be more important to you than other outcomes, so you would assign it a value of 100. Don't worry about being overly precise in doing this. It matters little if you assign a very important outcome a value of 90 or 100. After you assign each outcome a value, add up the values to get the total score of positive and negative outcomes for that choice.

4. To arrive at a decision, you would pick the choice that has the highest total positive outcome score. However, it is probably wise not to try to make your decision the first time you do this exercise. It is best to do the exercise and put your notebook away for some time. After that time, review what you have done and consider redoing the exercise, but without looking at the original one. The point here is you make sure you have made the best decision, and the best way to ensure you have is to arrive at the same choice on more than one occasion.

Table 10.2 shows what a completed worksheet would look like for the choice of quitting your job. Adding up the values we assigned to each outcome results in a total score of 210 for the positive outcomes and 280 for negative outcomes. As such, the negatives of just quitting outright are higher than the positives, so you would discard this as a choice.

Table 10.2.   Choice—Quit Your Job

Positive Outcome	0–100	Negative Outcome	0–100
Removed from the negative situation	70	Loss of income	100
Have time to look for a new job	40	Loss of friends at the job	30
More time with family and friends	60	Stress on relationships due to fewer financial resources	70
More time to do what I like	40	Fewer activities due to reduced financial resources	80

With respect to irrational beliefs about making decisions, you will generally find that some of these will come to the surface as you review and repeat this exercise. The most common irrational belief is that there is one perfect or best choice. You might be thinking, *There must be a perfect solution, why can't I find it? And if I can't find it, how can I make a decision?* The perfect choice rarely, if ever, is available, and a belief that one exists can lead to indecision because we keep searching for that perfect solution.

If you come across irrational beliefs in the decision process, take the time to refute these beliefs and replace them with ones that are more rational. That should speed up the decision and leave you more satisfied with your choices. You will also find that as you improve your decision-making skills, you will feel less intimidated and overwhelmed by the prospect of having to choose; you will feel as though you have taken back some control of your life.

A FEW FINAL THOUGHTS

So after you have put in place all of these guidelines, you're ready to live perfectly, right? Well, not really. There is no such thing as perfect when it comes to human beings. The road to psychological well-being has no final destination. It's about a journey that has no end (except the grave, but that's a topic for another book). While we are living, there is always room for improvement; we can always try to be better than we are, to feel more comfortable in our skins, and be more in control of our lives.

The fact that we never really arrive at our destination should not make you feel disillusioned. Instead, be proud of yourself for deciding to get on the road. You can take solace in the fact that you are trying to be a better person, that you are learning to dodge the various pitfalls and problems that come along. Eventually, with practice and effort, you will come to feel more in control and achieve more satisfaction in your day-to-day living.

As you move forward, keep reminding yourself to be patient. Change comes slowly and don't expect magic or rapid improvement. We all know that Rome wasn't built in a day. (In fact, Rome kept reinventing itself and trying to be a better city right up to its fall.) Remember too that change follows a sawtoothed curve. You'll make some progress and then you'll take a few steps backward. This is normal, so don't beat yourself up when you backslide. You will make mistakes as you go, but if you keep trying, you will eventually see results.

Don't try to change more than one thing at a time when you first get started on this path. Each of us has a lot we'd like to change about ourselves and it rarely comes down to just one thing. Your first goal is to prioritize what you'd like to work on. Find the one issue that you feel would have the most impact on your life, or the one that may be easiest to fix, and focus your attention just on that. Note that of these two options, we recommend going with the easier problem to fix. This can build your confidence because you have a better chance of being successful. As you make progress in this area, you can add another, but don't stop working on your first priority.

Above all, remember that self-reflection and self-monitoring are the key tools for change. Only through introspection can you truly come to know yourself. Only by building your self-awareness can you gain the insight you need to take charge of your life and improve your interactions with others and the world around you. Keep working at it and improvements will come.

As a closing remark, we have to point out that there is no such thing as a cure-all. The approaches we have outlined throughout each chapter might not work on every situation you face. Some problems may require a different approach while others may be better dealt with through professional assistance. Nevertheless, it can be helpful for quite a few problems. As its greatest benefit, it can reduce the intensity of your emotional reactions, and its applicability cuts across a broad range of life's obstacles. In fact, you might find that such techniques as rational emotive therapy are only limited by how creative you are in applying them.

APPENDIX

Recommended Readings

Alberti, R., and M. Emmons. *Your Perfect Right: Assertiveness and Equality in Your Life and Relationships*, 8th ed. Atascadero, CA: Impact Publishers, 2001.

Ellis, A. *Ask Albert Ellis: Straight Answers and Sound Advice from America's Best-Known Psychologist*. Atascadero, CA: Impact Publishers, 2003.

Ellis, A. *How to Live With a Neurotic*. Chatsworth, CA: Wilshire Book Company, 1979.

Ellis, A. *How to Make Yourself Happy and Remarkably Less Disturbable*. Atascadero, CA: Impact Publishers, 1999.

Ellis, A. *How to Stubbornly Refuse to Make Yourself Miserable about Anything: Yes, Anything!*. Secaucus, NJ: Lyle Stuart, 2000.

Ellis, A. *A New Guide to Rational Living*. Chatsworth, CA: Wilshire Book Company, 1975.

Ellis, A. *Reason and Emotion in Psychotherapy, Revised and Updated*. Secaucus, NJ: Carol Publishing Group, 1994.

Ellis, A., and R. Harper. *A Guide to Rational Living*. Englewood Cliffs, NJ: Prentice-Hall, 1961.

INDEX

ABOUT THE AUTHORS

Louis H. Primavera, PhD, is a New York State licensed psychologist trained in behavior and rational emotive behavior therapies. He maintained a private practice for more than twenty-five years specializing in marriage counseling. Primavera is currently dean of the School of Health Sciences at Touro College. Previously he was dean of the Derner Institute of Advanced Psychological Studies at Adelphi University, and held the department chair and served as associate dean of the Graduate School of Arts and Sciences at St. John's University. As well he has held full-time faculty positions at Hofstra University, St. Francis College, and Molloy College. Primavera has published extensively in the social sciences, and his work has appeared in a number of prestigious professional journals of psychology. He was a consultant to the Department of Psychiatry and Behavioral Sciences at Memorial Sloan Kettering Cancer Center and has held a number of other consulting positions in medicine, business, and education. He has been a member of a number of professional organizations and has served as president of the Academic Division of the New York State Psychological Association, and the New York City Metro Chapter of the American Statistical Association.

Rob Pascale, PhD, founded Marketing Analysts, Inc, a quantitative market research company, in 1982. Pascale retired from full-time responsibilities at MAi in 2005 at the age of fifty-one. Throughout his twenty-five-year tenure as president of MAi, Pascale was directly involved in over five thousand research studies for more than fifty of the largest corporations in the world and has polled well over two million consumers.